THE LONE SURVIVOR

Statement of Purpose

The Holocaust spread across the face of Europe just a few decades ago. The brutality then unleashed is still nearly beyond comprehension. Millions of innocents—men, women and children—were consumed by its flames.

The goal of Holocaust Publications, a non-profit organization founded by survivors, is to publish and disseminate works on the Holocaust. These will include survivors' accounts, testimonies and memoirs, historical and regional analyses, anthologies, archival and source documents and other relevant materials that will help shed light on this cataclysmic era.

These books and studies will be made available to the general public, scholars, researchers, historians, teachers and students. They will be used in Holocaust Resource Centers, libraries and schools, synagogues and churches. They will help foster an increased awareness of the Holocaust and its implications. They will help to preserve the memory for posterity and to enable this awesome time to be better understood and comprehended.

Holocaust Library
216 West 18th Street
New York, NY 10011
212-463-7988

MICHAEL DIMENT
THE LONE SURVIVOR
A DIARY OF THE LUKACZE GHETTO AND SVYNIUKHY, UKRAINE

Translated by Shmuel (Diment) Yahalom

HOLOCAUST LIBRARY
NEW YORK

© 1992 by Michael Diment

Library of Congress Cataloging-in-Publication Data

Diment, Michael, 1915-
    The lone survivor : a diary of the Lukacze ghetto and Svyniukhy / by Michael Diment ; translated by Shmuel (Diment) Yahalom.
      p.   cm.
    Translation.
    ISBN 0-89604-152-2 (paperbk.) : $13.95
    1. Diment, Michael, 1915-   —Diaries. 2. Jews—Ukraine—Lokachi—Diaries. 3. Holocaust, Jewish (1939-1945)—Ukraine—Lokachi—Personal narratives. 4. World War, 1939-1945—Underground movements, Jewish—Ukraine. 5. Lokachi (Ukraine) —Ethnic relations.
    I. Title.
DS135.R93L6433   91-10994
940.53′18′0947718—dc20   CIP

Cover Design by The Appelbaum Company

Printed in the United States of America

*Dedicated to the victims of the Lukacze area —
their memory will remain with us forever.
To our wives — Lea and Chana.*

מוקדש לזכר קורבנות לוקאץ' וסביבותיה שנרצחו –
זכרונם יהיה אתנו לעד.
ומוקדש לנשותינו – לאה וחנה.

CONTENTS

Preface   ix

One   Introduction   1
Two   Power Transfer from the
Russian to the German Regime   3
Three   Life in the Lukacze
Ghetto and Svyniukhy   38
Four   The Slaughter of the
Lukacze Ghetto Inhabitants   106
Five   Life in the Forests
and Liberation   148

Appendix One   Map of the Region   220
Appendix Two   The Evolution of the Record-
Keeping of the Diary   222
Appendix Three   Explanation for the
Delay in Publication   223

PREFACE

The translation of my father's diary from Yiddish into English was extremely painful and emotionally depressing. For years I knew about its existence, but I was not allowed to read it. My parents wanted to shield me from their unprecedented experience. The story of ghettos and Nazis was in the background of all the years of my growing up in Israel. The details of my father's anguish were not fully revealed until I finished translating the diary.

The diary describes the events from the day the Germans invaded Lukacze and Svyniukhy (today the town is called Privetnyeh) on June 22, 1941 until liberation (April 16, 1944). It is unique in its detailed description of ghetto and peasant life in an area about which very little is known. The Ukraine before the war consisted of more than 5000 small Jewish communities of a few hundred inhabitants. These were wiped out by the Nazis, and their story will never be revealed. Some might even question their existence. The Lukacze ghetto numbered 1800 inhabitants who were gathered by the Germans from the surrounding villages. Before the slaughter, 700 were fortunate enough the war. Some succumbed to disease and/or extreme weather. The rest were murdered by the Germans and the Ukrainians in the forests.

The diary details the outrageous acts against human beings and their reactions in its full spectrum. The inhuman acts can be categorized into: personal suffering (emotional, wear-and-tear on the human mind, manipulations of the mind, illusions, fear, action and inaction, and more), mass population manipulation (raising hopes and dashing them, to name a few), economic decrees (dividing the population into economically valuable and economically worthless people, removing all tools from the ghetto to eliminate a possible self-defense move, as examples), historical data of all the events in the ghetto and in the area before and after the slaughter, political movements and thoughts (the Ukrainian movement for independence, gangs, whistle blowers and fears, to mention a few) and much more. The diary offers the opportunity for historians, economists, sociologists, psychologists, political scientists and the general public to glean a better understanding and more important data about human behavior under stressful conditions.

For me the information was shocking.

Shocking was the fact that nothing was done during the war to halt the outrageous act of destroying a very old culture responsible for so much good for humanity. Even more astonishing was the fact that after the war the victims were falsely stigmatized as ones who "went like sheep to the slaughter". The victims who survived were mistreated for a long time. The world refused to hear their story. A "conspiracy" of some sort, to silence them so that the conscience of those who did nothing while babies, children, women and the elderly were killed, would not be disturbed.

The victims' drive to survive was the desire to tell, erroneously believing that the world would want to know what happened, but it was disappointed again. The silent treatment the survivors received continued until their children progressed politically and economically and started to publish their parents' stories.

The fact that the criminal act of the destruction of a nation was conducted by other countries is still puzzling. The fact that people who knew the details of what was happening asked for help, without success, was, and still is, quite puzzling. That it was not covered in the western press, was, and still is, incomprehensible. The fact that the leaders of the world, Roosevelt, Churchill and Stalin, did nothing when they knew what was happening, was and still is, unbelievable.

The victims' message, "NEVER FORGET", is the universal slogan to remember.

The diary consists of five parts which are organized in chronological order. A few later additions are placed in brackets and noted as such. They were perceived initially to be unimportant, although they were recorded in the original entries. The names of towns are in Polish. Names of people are associated with their nationality. Included are a map of the area, an account of how the data was collected and an explanation for the delay in publication.

to escape, but only six survived to witness the end of

The success of the project is attributed to my wife who was the editor and a financial contributor as well, to my children who gave up much of their time with me for the project, to my parents for their financial support of the project and for their help at every step. Special thanks are acknowledged to Mr. and Mrs. Morton Meizlish for their financial support and encouragement. Also thanks for the monetary help of: Mr. and Mrs. Eli Freedman, Mrs. Jayne Lee, Mr. Julius Lichter, Mr. Harry Zemel, Mr. Milton Socolar, Mrs. Esther Zweig, Mrs. Lillian Schimberg and to the Charles and Els Bendheim Foundation, Jesselson Foundation, and the Svyniukhy Organization.

Shmuel Yahalom

ONE
INTRODUCTION

I should like to dedicate this diary to the memory of my family who were among the holy children of Israel who were killed.

In this introduction I have assumed the responsibility of giving a general overview of the diary, which was written under unusual and difficult circumstances, and at times under abnormal conditions.

The diary identifies a number of periods:

1. Transfer of power from the Russian to the German regime,
2. Life in the Lukacze (Eng. Lockachi) Ghetto,
3. The slaughter,
4. Life in the forests,
5. Liberation.

The time has passed, but the lives of the victims have not been invalidated. The victims for whom we are still saying Kaddish (prayer for the dead) are not almost forgotten. It is definite that the "forgetfulness minister" is very telented, forceful and strong. With the power of humor, he will forget and then absolve this reptile's crime.

2 *The Lone Survivor*

Two years have passed since the war. We have almost forgotten the Amalek who fulfilled Chmielnicki's wish. Two years after the war, I wonder if the echo of our feelings were heard in the various regimes of the world. The pain is not short-lived or accidental; it is one that transcends time. The source of the hurt started a long time ago and progressed to the yellow patch.

This diary must serve as a monument at a time of repentance, when human beings together with their loved ones were cold, weak, burned, and killed. This for the sanctification of the memory of the Jewish nation. In writing this diary, I accepted the responsibility of commemorating our holy ones from the Lukacze Ghetto and the general Jewish tragedy. This book is a memorial document for study by present and future generations, to remember the Nazi reptile and its avowed commitment to "extinguish our people from the face of the earth".

This book should provide an explanation about those weak characters who wanted to save themselves from destruction at the worst moments in their lives by using corrupt methods of bribing, becoming informants and resorting to other base methods. The memory of our dearest friends and family will remind us of our humanity and the nation to which we belong.

TWO
POWER TRANSFER FROM THE RUSSIAN TO THE GERMAN REGIME

Early on the beautiful summer morning of July 22, 1941, people gathered outside to listen to the noise coming from a distance. I heard people say, painfully: "Again a war". The Germans were attacking once more. Germany's attack on Russia took everyone by surprise.

Workers from the border between Russia and Germany returned to town. People gathered curiously to listen to every word of their stories and to hear every detail of the horrible and unexpected night incursion. We heard about the heavy bombardment of the working area, about confusion, about the helplessness of the sleeping guards and the officers. A high-ranking military official ordered all civilians and workers 18 years and older, to return to their home towns.

We left the border area quickly and proceeded toward Ludmir (Ger. Vladimir-Volynski, Pol. Wlodzimierz). When we arrived in Ludmir, the city was in flames from the German shelling. We continued towards our town. Moving along the road was quite difficult with so many people there! We passed many, most of them young and frightened. The fear was unbearable and indescribable. Suddenly, we saw Walkie Niticuk (an official from the town committee in Svyniukhy); all eyes turned toward him as he sadly said "Yes, my friends, we have a war." He asked us to come to the club at seven o'clock for a meeting. He urged all to participate.

The town was becoming crowded with people from everywhere. They were mostly women. Among them were many wives and children of the soldiers at the front. All those that arrived told similar stories about bombs and shells falling everywhere. The town of Poryck (Eng. Poritzk) was burning, destroyed. As the wounded arrived, a woman screamed, "The enemy will pay heavily. Russia will never surrender, Napoleon was soundly defeated in the Russian mud and so will Hitler's army be decimated here."

A young person holding a sign turned to us and asked if he could attend the meeting. We moved to the meeting hall as one. We noticed that the people there came from all over the area. The crowd was large and were mostly Ukrainian. Near the entrance we heard a shout, "Quiet". All eyes turned to the stage to see Walkie Niticuk and two others. Walkie broke the silence; "Friends, workers, intellectuals and *kolchoz* (commune) members; hard times have overtaken us. The sky is black and the enemy is prepared to destroy us. We strove always for peace. We did everything to maintain peace and to prevent a disaster. While the world was bleeding we stood aside, but the war did not pass us by. However the day has come. We had to get involved to destroy Fascism. When we were attacked, we offered no resistance. Now the Communist Party led by Comrade Stalin has decided to thrust the power of the Red Army into the war. From today on, no one is allowed to leave his home unless he or she is carrying out a mission." The meeting was adjourned and the communist party members remained.

The normal quiet of the evenings were shattered by the continuous sound of airplanes flying above us. Unrest was pervasive. People could not sleep; they waited in fear, wondering what tomorrow would bring. Then Szurko Trufimyuck showed up and delivered military mobilization orders for me, Avraham Schwartz and other friends. At 6 AM we were to be at the club.

Early in the morning the newly mobilized started to gether. By horse and buggy, peasants arrived accompanied by their wives, parents and children; crying, whining and moaning filled the air. Drinking, singing and dancing were the last manifestations of anticipation. Promptly at 7:30 AM, a delegation led by the mayor with a few others appeared; they wandered somberly and quietly among the people and left without uttering a word.

The crowd formed into small groups, discussing their ideas and opinions about the events. Suddenly, Laib Briger, sweaty from running, shouted, "It's all over. The Germans have moved into Lukacze. The city is already closed. The Russians in Koslov are fleeing to the wheat fields. Shainer's (a mill) is in flames. The Germans are expected here at any hour."

Walkie Niticuk came to tell all who were mobilized, to go home. If they needed us, they would let us know. The assembled slowly dispersed and went home. Those who stayed were local Jews and Ukrainians. In some isolated areas of town a few small "local" Ukrainian farmers remained, conversing in their local dialect;

they repeated that they had heard, that "the Germans are not so bad".

Shortly afterwards Avraham Lichter reported that the Germans were in town and that Froika Meizlish saw them and even talked with them. They were near the cooperative store (town store), from which they took chocolate and cotton. They used the cotton upon which to sleep at the school. They stayed in town for the night.

Evening was approaching. Most people stayed indoors. A few families gathered for the night, sharing all kinds of views. No one really knew what to expect.

In the morning, the town was quaking from the shelling. Germans were ordering people to carry water, shine shoes, and to obey their commands.

Within a few hours the German soldiers left town. As soon as this was done, a few of us gathered in Bella Meizlish's house to exchange first impressions from the short stay of the Germans. As we were sitting there, we heard noises. German soldiers returned. Four of them entered and asked for soda. While Bela was serving, between talking and drinking, they said that it would not be much longer before they would finish the dumb Russians, then the English and the Americans. This would bring the war to an early end and fulfill their dream of conquering the world.

The fields looked black viewing the German soldiers' uniforms, as they moved away. The sounds continued until noon, at which time it became quiet. A few of us met in the house of Yecheskel Greenspan, spontaneously discussing the situation in light of the new developments. After a short respite, the sound of Germans in transit prevailed. The soldiers entered every house, asking for eggs and butter which were in short supply. Many soldiers just appropriated whatever they wanted. We heard the sound of shooting everywhere, but we did not know who the perpetrators were.

It was evening again. We locked and nailed the doors shut in our house and went to sleep at the Greenspans, where a few families had congregated. The quiet of the night was disturbed by the continual shooting of flare rockets that lit the sky and surrounding areas and the explosions of mines. Close in the dark, we all sat on the floor. The quiet crying and sobbing of women was heard long into the night. At the first signs of dawn, we slowly looked outside to see what was happening in the street. When meeting neighbors, the usual questions were, "How are you?" and "Were you robbed"? In many homes the Nazis stole everything they could find.

The German military prepared to march forward with all their equipment. They were moving without stop. Every available area in town was occupied by the German military.

When my father and I returned to our house, we found all the doors broken. The Germans were removing everything. Two soldiers jumped at us, screaming sarcastically, "Jews? Jews? They should be killed", directed mostly to my father, because his beard betrayed his Jewishness. I gave them eggs and butter and they left. We decided to leave everything as it was, and went to Yecheskel. Robbery in town was a common occurrence, and many Jews were badly beaten. Panic was spreading like a raging fire and Jews ran to the village peasants for protection.

In town, only ten Jewish families remained on the side of the bridge where Yecheskel and his brother, Meir, lived. An unknown Jew and a young girl, with torn and dirty clothes, came in. Yecheskel received them warmly with a *"Shalom aleichem"* and asked, "How did you get here in such a hazardous time?" The stranger looked around, checking if there were any soldiers about. Fearfully, he told us that on the first day of the war, the Russians shot down a German pilot. On the following day, when the Germans arrived, the Ukrainians spread the canard that the Jews were responsible. The Germans tortured some Jews, then killed them. A day later, another German unit came, surrounded the town of Ozdziutycze (Eng. Odziutichi, Uk. Ozdziutyeze) near Poritzk, rounded up all the Jews, selected 80 men, shot them and burned the town. If they encountered any others in the town, they killed them, as well.

The population of the area was reduced to women and children only. Fearful because of our close proximity to Odziutichi, we fled into the wheat fields and towards the neighboring farms. We decided to keep going, despite the imminent dangers and difficulties posed by the soldiers on the road. We met many scared women and children. Bairel's descriptions of the events in Odziutichi made many women cry. Yecheskel was trying to calm them down so the Nazis would not hear the clamor.

The German army curtailed its movements. Valvel Briger returned to town. When he came back, he described the wanton destruction; everything was demolished or vandalized, especially entire households.

The Jews who had been hiding started to return to

town. We pressed them for all the details of the events that transpired in the last few days.

On June 27 at 4 PM German military trucks rolled through town. The noise of artillery firing was quite loud; the battle was very near. Some saw German trucks with soldiers lying on top of each other, screaming horribly. One car was dripping blood. The trucks transported wounded and dead.

The fighting did not subside at night, and rockets illuminated the windows. In the morning the peasants from the neighboring towns told us that the Red Army was battling the Germans near the Korytnytsia forest. The Germans occupied a few houses in town, examined the population and moved on. It was quiet, and peasants were visible once again. In this environment on a Friday evening, the Shabbat candles were lit.

Saturday, at 11 AM we heard shooting close by. A short time later a Red Army soldier appeared. "Are there any German soldiers here?" he asked. Many units of the Russian armed forces appeared. They happily declared that they had beaten the dirty Nazis. The Russian soldiers, barefoot and ragged, were asking for water. All they drank did not seem to quench their thirst. They refused to accept any bread.

A low-flying German plane attacked the Red Army units. The soldiers returned fire with full power. The aircraft was hit and crashed aflame in a nearby field. The Russians left town and headed towards Korytnytsia. The burning plane was the latest topic of conversation. A short time later a few Germans came, buried the pilot and marked the grave with his helmet.

The movement of armed forces stopped. It was quiet once more. Small groups met to discuss the transition.

10   The Lone Survivor

(No superpower authority had as yet been established; Russian or German.) We heard that in the last two days, a number of people had been killed, including Laib Briger and an unknown person from Svyniukhy, and that the last units of the German army that passed through the region, were responsible.

We heard from other towns in the area, that the Ukraine had become an independent state and that they assumed the responsibility for law and order. We learned from Lukacze that the Ukrainians were coming our way to organize the local administration.

On July 7, Ukrainian teen-agers were calling everyone to a meeting in the public school. A large crowd assembled, including peasants from nearby villages. On stage prominently displayed were a German flag and a Ukrainian one. A member of the trio unfamiliar to me on the dais started with "Today we are marching into the history of the liberation of the Ukrainian people. We owe thanks to our leaders; Hitler and Bandero. We are finally declaring our independence like many other nations. We have paid for our freedom with a great deal of blood. We have lost too many sons for the *Zhydy* (Jews in the Ukraine). We were victorious with the Jewish communists. Our fighters are moving forward. Kiev has been taken. The great Fuhrer has undertaken the task of annihilating the *Zhydivs'ka Kommuna* (Jewish communists) outcasts within six weeks, and Jewish rule will be broken once and for all. After finishing with the outcasts, we will concentrate our efforts to destroy the Jewish leadership in England and America as well. Look around," he said (pointing to where, on the 27th, 12 Germans were buried after dying in Korytnytsia), "our best and bravest sons are dying for the freedom of our people.

"Now we will have an election for the Committee and police. Only our brothers have the right to be elected, no foreigners. It is enough that until now all key positions were held by the Jews. From now their rights are rescinded. They cannot become workers and they will not be offered any jobs. From today on, they are not allowed to attend school; they will be punished if they do. Our children's blood is still fresh, and cry for revenge, not tears."

Andrii Bahmet was elected Chairman of the local village committee, and Oleksander Zawads'kyi was chosen to become the chief of police. These actions brought the meeting to an end.

Gathered happily in small groups, the Ukrainians discussed the events that took place. No Jews were in sight; they were all indoors, with their entire families gathered to discuss the events. In general, it seemed as if everything was at a standstill, with no jobs available and no way to earn a living.

After the Red Army left, many Ukrainians dressed as NKVD (Russian secret police). Our Jewish sons who fought for our freedom and were jailed were now slaughtered in prison by those NKVD. In Lutsk alone 18 men were killed, and so it was in other towns throughout the Ukraine. The Jewish population which was spread all over, started to leave, moving cautiously far from the main roads.

Jewish refugees were passing through our area. They were invited into Jewish homes and were helped, commensurate with the host's ability. We had to improvise to stave off hunger. Those from Odziutichi suffered most. People from Poritzk were more fortunate; they, at least, were alive. Inhabitants of the cities of Ludmir (Wladimir Wolynsk or in Polish Wlodzimierz) and Lutsk suffered, too. Hunger became rampant when Jews were forbidden to buy from farmers in the villages. It was even dangerous to go to the farm. (The peasants were the source of virtually all agricultural products. Some, who worked for Jews would, sometimes during the night, bring in some produce.)

At 10 AM on July 9, an announcement summoned all Jews to the synagogue to hear a statement from Zawads'kyi. Shortly afterwards he arrived, accompanied by Wici Bodj, and said, "I called you to make it clear that what I have to say is not of my own volition. I received orders. From today on you do not participate in the general elections. You have to have a separate one for your own leaders and police. Those who are voted in, will serve as contacts between you and us. You can elect whoever you wish."

We chose Yecheskel Greenspan and Yitzhak Pechornik, and Zawads'kyi recorded it. Wici Bodj said, "Since we are here, I would like to tell you that starting tomorrow, every man, woman and child, without exception, will have to wear a *Mogen Dovid* (six-pointed star) ribbon. Without it you cannot appear on the street. In addition, it is imposed on your town, and you have to comply by tomorrow, to submit 110 kilos of sugar, 2 kilos of pepper and 400 kilos of high-grade flour. As you also know, you cannot venture outside after 7 PM, and you must not have any contact with the Christian population."

Yecheskel and Yitzhak Pechornik collected the required items. Getting the sugar was somewhat difficult, but by exchanging among us we obtained what was needed. All wore the ribbons. Jews who were deported from the surrounding towns came in. The orders issued on the previous day stipulated that members of Jewish families who were not born or who settled in town after the last war, would have to leave by 10 AM, July 12, the following day.

Yecheskel announced that we must send as many people as were needed for work. Yecheskel and Yitzhak listed all the able-bodied people ages 18 to 54 who had to report for a work detail, without exceptions. On July 13, the first group of 30 were sent, men to repair roads, women to clean town installations and the young to cut wood for the peasants. When the workers returned they said that the labor itself was not that terrible, but that the worst thing of all was the degradation inflicted on us by the peasants.

These would come from the area to the work locations in town to beat the Jews, some were quite brutal. When the victims returned home covered with blood, people panicked.

The news from the region was not pleasant. Terror was rampant. Beside those forced to labor, people did nothing. Professionals and craftsmen, who were mostly Jews, were unemployed, although there was a shortage of their skills. The sight of the idle ones made the peasants terribly angry.

On July 17, 1941, Yecheskel and Yitzhak Pechornik were called before the town council. They were told that from the following day on, all artisans and professionals would have to return to their designated jobs, for which they would be paid in cash, but at a reduction of 50% from the wages in normal times. Payment in goods was not allowed. Posters announcing the lower payment and none in kind, were posted with a warning that violators would be brought before the police. The town was revived for Jew and gentile alike. Gentiles once again stopped by Jewish homes, but inside we were still fearful for our safety, as we sensed something dreadful was immiment, no one knew what or when. People gathered at Yecheskel's house nervously waiting, but they did not know for what.

On July 19, Yecheskel was summoned by a militiaman. Upon returning, he called everyone to a meeting in the synagogue. At which time Yecheskel announced that the district commissar (a German) from Horochow (Eng. Gorokhov, Uk. Horokhiv) had just decreed that all gold and silver would be confiscated and turned in to the district commissar by July 21. Anyone not complying and found in possession of gold or silver would be shot immediately. We started to collect, and Yecheskel kept a record of what people contributed. The vast majority brought jewelry that had been in the family for many generations; all together 435 pieces were collected.

On July 21, Yecheskel and Zawads'kyi went to turn the jewelry over to the district commissar. We all waited anxiously for their return. At 4 PM they came back. Yecheskel was apprehensive. We were waiting for some news, but he had nothing to say.

The Jews in town were in a panic. We heard about the surprise visits by the Gestapo, who would kidnap Jews, young and intelligent, and claim that they were taking them for work. Others received no explanation, they were just killed.

Life became easier to a degree because some Jews were toiling for the committee. But the situation posed a dilemma. The order prohibited craftsmen and professionals to register for unskilled labor, but the craftsmen and professionals unskilled quotas had to be filled anyway.

On July 22, Germans came into town, and a militiaman called for Yecheskel. By 11 AM he was back with a new decree; a demand for 100 kilos of sugar, 500 kilos of flour and other materials that had to be collected. Yecheskel and Pechornik gathered all of it by 4 PM and it was taken away by car.

Early on July 23, Yecheskel was summoned again. Embittered, he returned with the message that the district commissar demanded that all horses and wagons be confiscated and turned over to the local peasants. Many Jewish sources of income were eliminated, and the situation worsened. The *Judenrat* (Jewish Council), including Yecheskel and Pechornik, tried to intervene pleading that the Jewish farmers who owned land would not be able to harvest the fields; the answer they received was that the peasants would make it possible for them to reap their harvest.

The town was in a turmoil. Confiscations were carried out by the militia and other lackeys, all of whom were at the helm. They seized all the horses and wagons that belonged to the Jews. They were supposedly looking for parts for the wagons, in the yards, but, while they were at it, they appropriated all other wares; virtually everything was taken. The peasants fought over the division of the loot.

The town looked as if it had suffered a pogrom. Traffic among the cities and the small towns was halted and so were communications. Normally, men did not commute a great deal because they feared kidnaping by the Gestapo; women did most of the traveling.

The militia men in the villages were beating Jews whenever they met them. The situation was getting worse daily; the pressure was mounting. The terror was perpetrated by the militia of neighboring villages as well. Yankel Lichter and Zalman Linver were kidnaped by them, taken out of town and ordered to lay on the ground and eat the grass like cattle. When they refused, they were severely beaten. The militia also siezed Maite Fichman and Munia Finkel; by evening they had not returned. The next morning (July 24) Yecheskel went to the commissariat. At 8 AM they all returned exhausted and bruised from the torture inflicted upon them. They reported that for 45 minutes they were pounded in jail by the Germans because under the Russian regime they indulged in too much dancing.

Surprisingly, Avraham Wallach was summoned to the town committee in the Lukacze area. When a day had passed and he was not back, his wife Riva with her two brothers, Avraham and Aaron Lichter, went to Lukacze to find out what had happened.

That same evening (July 25), spent and weak, Riva collapsed entering the house. She reported today's slaughter in Lukacze, and the murder of her two brothers. She observed the terrible fear that was rampant in the town, and all the stores that were closed. Lukacze was surrounded by Gestapo and Ukrainian police and they were looking for men. People were hiding in every place possible, even in the chimneys. Those who were caught were severely beaten and were gathered near the hospital were later only a large pit and some pickaxes were found.

The news spread quickly. We all had but one thought; where to hide when the Gestapo appeared. We realized that every one looked out for himself, keeping his plans secret. Most people began to build bunkers for themselves and their family, only relatives knew where, small children did not. When the Germans arrived in town, the young children acted as spies watching their movements, craftsmen, while working kept a watchful eye, women remained at home in readiness. Everyone was very nervous.

The Jews' life entered a critical stage. The Ukrainians did what they pleased; killing a Jew was not punishable. The circumstances required finding ways of bribing the town committee and the police for some security. The problem with bribery was that it never ended, and even then it might not save anyone.

In town, Yecheskel bought all sorts of things, mostly cloth and leather products, which were given to the chief of police Zawads'kyi, chairman of the town and his deputy Wici Bodj. Zawads'kyi announced that the Svyniukhy Jews were under his protection and that the Svyniukhy police and those in the area, had no right to beat the Jews. In any dispute with local Jews, they should turn to the town committee for help.

On July 31 I was working with my father when two policemen, Sandyk Iwankis and one I didn't know entered, turned to my father and asked him to accompany them to the police. After a fast change of clothes, he joined them. I immediately left for the police building to see my father. There I turned to Zawads'kyi, and asked him where my father was. He did not answer. I asked the militiaman: "Where is my father?" "Down in the basement, in jail, and I don't know anything else," he said. I tried to get down to the jail when I was stopped and thrown back. I confronted Zawads'kyi again and asked for permission to see my father. After pleading to visit with my father, he allowed me to see him through the basement window for 10 minutes. I called, "Father, Father". He recognized my voice and asked me to come closer to the small window at which he was sitting. "What did they tell you?" he inquired. "Nothing," I replied. He said he was told that on the next day early in the morning he would be taken to Horochow. That was all he knew. He asked me for warm clothing for the night and added that I should decide what action to take. The militiaman shouted that my time was up, hit me with his gun, and I left.

The arrest of my father caused a big commotion in town. Why arrest a 62-year-old talented craftsman? I brought everything my father requested for his stay in jail, and went to Yecheskel.

He told me that they learned about the arrest and that they were trying to get him released. I accompanied Yecheskel to Zawads'kyi's home. I stayed outside while Yecheskel went in. After a long while, he came out, and told me that Zawads'kyi would not release him. Yecheskel promised Zawads'kyi a new suit and leather for boots, but it did not help. Zawads'kyi claimed that my father had committed too many sins, and that he had to take him to the governor in Horochow. We went to Andrii and to Wici Bodj offering them gifts and pleaded, but to no avail. The night passed. By eight o'clock in the morning people were

Power Transfer to the German Regime 19

looking through their windows. A wagon with two policemen and my father between them passed. I ran towards the vehicle shouting to my father that we were doing everything possible to help him.

My father's situation did not improve. The promises of payoffs were becoming intensified; everyone was on the take. They all guaranteed to get my father released, but we never knew if they really meant it or could, in fact, succeed. I gave Zawads'kyi what I said I would but he was not the only one. Everyone wanted a piece of the pie.

The farmers said that he could obtain my father's release because his outstanding abilities as a blacksmith were needed.

My sister Batia and my aunt Rachel went to Horochow every day. There, it was very difficult to find out what was happening. The utensils on which they served food to my father were returned empty.

On August 2 the town was in a state of a turmoil. The militia imposed a curfew. Yecheskel told us that they were searching homes for arms and encouraged us not be scared. The real reason for this search was apparent; they were appropriating leather, material or anything they liked. The militia released the town at noon on the following day. The robbery of the Jews in town brought an outcry by the local Ukrainian leadership.

The promise to release my father was not fulfilled. It was a cruel lie. One person that could have helped was the priest, Ritz Spatachnko, because he exerted some influence. I went to see him. "What is it, Diment?" he asked. "I think you know the reason I am here," I replied. "You know that my father was arrested, but we do not know why," I explained. "I would appreciate your help in this matter. You are a believer, a person with a heart and a conscience. I do not want to bother you, but now, I have no choice. I have tried everyone else. You are my last hope. Your involvement can change everything. I understand that it is difficult for you to intercede in this matter." He looked at me and said quietly, "Your father was arrested because he told a Ukrainian, whose name is not important, that the time of Petlura is coming back. Today to say that is an unforgivable big sin. You know what Petlura represented for the Ukrainians and you are aware who destroyed him. Stay strong; we will do all we can to obtain your father's release. Yesterday I spoke with all of our directors. I know that it cost you a great deal. They only laugh at you. Go home and rest; we hope that everything will turn out all right".

My sister Batia returned from Horochow and told us that in town there lived a girl named Siandele who was known to all. She was close to the German chief of police, visiting him every day. Maybe she would help. Many were suspicious of her because she made promises to many Jews whose relatives were in jail in Horochow, and not even one was released.

On August 5 we went to Horochow, arriving at 9:00 AM. The town was eerily quiet, as if it were one large cemetery. We called on Bela Zuker, and after some discussion she went to get Siandele. They returned after a short while. Before I could say anything, Siandele asked: "You are Hershel Diment's children?". "Yes," we replied. Your father has been in jail for so many days and you did not come to me? I am the only one who knows the chief of police so well!

I spend every night with him, I can get anything I want from him . . ." She went on and on. "Today I will resolve the problem of your father, but it will cost you a great deal of material and leather, . . ." she carried on. Her talk sounded incredible. Then she said, "So, what are you willing to give? Why are you sitting so quietly?" I answered, "Tomorrow, after my father is released, nothing will be too hard to come by." "Tonight I will arrange it, during the day I cannot do anything," she said.

Outside, the sky was cloudy. Batia followed me. We were afraid that I would be caught. My thoughts were only about ways I could free my father, when suddenly someone called: "Mechel, Mechel!" As if waking from a dream, I looked around and saw the priest nearby. He shook my hand and said, "What is new?" "Nothing," I replied. He told me that he arrived on his bycicle, and that he wondered how he could return because of the expected rain. I turned to him, "Dear priest, you are overly concerned about the rain. Let's talk about more important things like you know what." He shook my hand firmly. "I am going to talk with the commissar. Let's hope for the best," he said.

It arted to rain, and we came back to Bela. Sitting at the table, I fell asleep. When the rain stopped, Batia woke me and we went outside, hoping to see the priest and to learn what happened. After walking a few steps in the street, we heard a low voice calling, "Batia, Batia!" We looked around and again "Batia!" He turned and screamed, "father, father". We ran to him. He was leaning against the wall, and turning to us and in almost a whisper said, "Take me. I am too weak. I cannot walk". We took him and slowly walked to Bela's and laid him on a bed. He was seriously hurt with black-and-blue marks all over his face, hands and feet. His bloody clothes stuck to his body. Bela got a doctor immediately. He examined my father, murmuring to himself, "How can they do a thing like this?" The doctor said that my father's health was not too bad, that he was beaten severely but that his wounds were only external.

The news of my father's release spread through town. Women and children whose fathers were in jail entered the room where my father was lying; they looked and cried. The scene was difficult to bear. The comments heard were, "So this is what they are doing to our beloved children and fathers! Death would be much better."

My father slowly started to talk about the events of those imprisonment days. "On the first day I was put in jail, I was taken to a room in which all the doors and windows were shut. I was asked my name. Then, 'You don't like Petlura? He should have killed all of you. We will show you.' They beat me on the head with a gun and I lost consciousness. When I recovered, I was laying on a wet floor with a bucket of water near me and my body severely beaten. On the following day I felt sick; my entire body was wracked with pain. They gave me food. I recognized that it was from home, but I could not eat it. All day long militiamen were ordering me to jump. If you didn't, they would beat you. On the third day the events of the first day were repeated. At the end of the day, I could not stand up. At 11:00 AM I was called into a room. Sitting alone I heard them talking about me in another room. I did not recognize the voice, but it sounded familiar. The commander entered and asked me if I liked Petlura. They removed my shoes, laid me down on a table and hit me 25 times with a rubber hose. I lost consciousness. When I regained it, two militiamen who had stayed in the room told me that I could leave. I could not stand. They helped me up, brought me over to the door and said, 'Now run.'"

Noisily, the door opened. Siandele entered. Everyone was observing her. She was talking endlessly: "I, only I, can do everything". I looked into her face; she seemed wild and aggressive. "In short, what do you want?" I asked. "What do you mean what do I want? You promised that you would reward me, and that nothing would be too hard to come by! What, am I not entitled to anything?" Bela took her into another room and they came to some agreement. However, we realized that it was the priest, not Siandele, who was responsible for the release.

At 4:00 PM we returned home, hungry and tired. When we arrived in town, everyone already knew that my father was free. I learned from Yecheskel that the priest reported seeing my father after his release, but moving slowly, holding onto the walls, not knowing where he was or where he was going.

The torture my father suffered wrought panic and fear in town. We were terrorized daily. We tried to devise ways to avoid being kidnaped or disappearing after being seized by the police or the Gestapo.

The population in our town increased daily with an influx of people from Horochow and other towns, many needing help. Yecheskel kept a list of the newcomers, between the ages of 18 and 55, classified as either professionals or unskilled laborers. Quite a lot registered as professionals, who were believed to be more appreciated and thus to have a better chance for survival, even though some had academic degrees. In spite of the difficulties in our small town, we tried to supply jobs for as many as possible.

On August 7 Yecheskel and Pechornik were summoned to the police. A number of people gathered in Yecheskel's house awaiting the news. After a few hours Yecheskel and Pechornik returned and requested that all those who had the time, gather in the house. It became crowded quickly. They reported in detail about the lengthy meeting with Zawads'kyi and Wici Bodj. The town officials revealed what we knew for a long time: in all the towns of Wolynia kidnapings by the Gestapo were taking place, and the Gestapo asked about our town. The town officials stated, though it was hard to believe, that there were only 360 Jews in our town and that all the men were professionals who were responsible for its daily economic activity. The officials promised to watch us. They continued that there were also a large number of unknown Jewish refugees from the surrounding area afraid of remaining in their own homes. These, they claimed, might be communists or criminals. They therefore declared that these must leave immediately. Anyone caught hiding refugees would be severely punished.

The new decrees caused much bitterness. Among the people ordered to leave were many relatives, and how can one suddenly tell small children and women, having recently lost their fathers and husbands, to go? They were hungry and possessed only the clothes on their backs. As the news spread, the refugees very quickly took their children and left. There was a great deal of crying. Some stayed anyway, because it was very difficult to ask them to go. We gave the refugees who left town, food and other useful items, as much as they were able to carry.

Working conditions worsened. Every militiaman who had some connections was getting as many Jews as he wanted to do the dirty or heavy work in his home or farm. Even though this was happening, the general feeling was that it was better to be in the fields with the peasants; if the need arose, it would be easier to escape from a sudden Gestapo assault. Jews who owned land slept in the field at night because they were afraid.

The demand for workers increased, but there were not enough available. Professionals were not allowed to handle unskilled jobs which meant that the unskilled had to work very hard, sometimes non-stop for 24 hours.

On August 9, men were fleeing because many unknown militiamen appeared in town. We did not know why or what was happening. Panic gripped everyone. Before leaving, I told my sister Chaike that my friends and I would lie in the pits on the hill near Andrii. I asked her to keep us informed about what was happening.

After a few hours Chaike, very frightened, asked us to return home. "The militia had gone. They arrested Shlomo Gorenstain and Avraham Schwartz and took them to Horochow," she told us. The town looked as if it had suffered a huge disaster. Women were crying, "We will never see them again, such young men!"

When we entered Yecheskel's house, if was filled

with people. The two women whose husbands had been arrested asked Yecheskel to do everything possible to obtain their husbands' releases. The militiamen initially had also arrested Sander Schochet and Yankel Lichter. The priest interceded for Sander and Yankel and they were released. For the two others it was impossible. Shlomo Gorenstain, during the Soviet takeover, was a bank director and Avraham Schwartz, a committee representative. Shlomo's arrest brought great sadness to the community because he was very popular among the Jews.

Yecheskel began to feel helpless. He did not trust the murderers. He spoke openly: "After every incident, I am forced to run and intercede. You know how much we gave them already? Who can we blame for all the arrests if not the Ukrainians? If they did not relish terror and arrests, they wouldn't happen. Their action is our daily curse. When I go to the Ukrainians after each incident, I am received with cynical laughter. They pretend they had nothing to do with the particular incident. The Ukrainians can control their own activities, but not those of the Germans."

When Shlomo and Avraham were arrested, the local police beat them mercilessly. When Shlomo was lying on the ground, bleeding, they did not stop; they cruelly said: "Oh yes, we have to save them!"

The town Jews, together with the ones from Horochow and the priest, attempted to gain freedom for the arrested. The priest was afraid for his life. We sent him anything he wanted, asking only that he do something for those incarcerated. It became quite complicated. The use of terror became a daily event. Life became unbearable.

On August 11 I was called to the town council. There, Wici Bodj turned to me and said: "When your father was in jail, we said nothing. Peasants are complaining that their work is not done. We want you to start tomorrow morning. Otherwise, we have ways about which you already know." I replied that I didn't have coal and files, so I would not be able to work. "For coal, we will give you a requisition for the regional commissioner in Horochow; after he signs it, you will get your coal. Tomorrow you have to bring it and start to work," he said. They gave me the document and I left.

August 12 in the morning a peasant came to escort me. I climbed into the wagon with my aunt Rachel. She joined us to make sure that nothing would happen to me. On the road we met Fraidel Schochet, Shlomo Gorenstain's wife, and Riva Schwartz; we discussed their husbands' arrests.

When we came to Skubelki, a suburb of Horochow, we encountered Germans going to Horochow in two cars and a truck. When they arrived, I immediately went to get the paper signed. The commissioner did so and added a printed note in German. Before handing me the ticket, he held it in his hand, about to say something. He kept nervously glancing out of the window, as if he was wondering whether to tell me something, but he kept quiet. He returned the signed document and told me to go.

Outside there was a great deal of noise. As I stepped out, I saw Jews with pickaxes being pushed around in the street. Using back roads, I got closer, when, suddenly, a militiaman shouted: "Come, *Zhyd.*" I showed him my note, but he refused to let me go. Our group of

Jews was being jostled by Germans and militiamen. A German called me to him, so I showed him the note; after carefully examining it, he hit me on the back with a rubber club. Returning the paper, he told me to get on the line. The Jews were gathered in small groups which were then merged into larger ones. Children were running after their parents, holding onto their clothes while the Germans were beating their mothers and fathers. Many children tried to give small packages to their parents but they were stopped. All this was happening while we were marching out of town into a large enclosed yard. There were about 70 men there already, guarded by five Gestapos who were walking around and one more who was using a typewriter. Three men with picks were taken over to the registration table. After they were processed, they formed a line and a German announced: "Thirty-eight men are leaving with us." To this group he said: "If anyone of you tries to escape, you will be shot on the spot". Two young guards with machine guns accompanied the group, one walking in front and the other in the rear. The group left. The selections continued; we were standing in line and were permitted to move. Even going to the toilet was done under the watchful eye of a guard. The noise continued. A steady stream of people was being brought in, some of them badly beaten and covered with blood.

The line moved slowly. I was able to hear the typewriter. More people came in. The militiamen were bragging to the Germans: "We dragged Jews out from cellars, from under beds and other hiding places. We know how to handle them!" It was my turn at the registration table. The German shouted: "What is your name?" "Diment Michael," I answered. "What is your birth date?" he continued. After I answered all of his questions, I asked, in German, for permission to show him my "ticket". He examined it, screamed something, pointed to the left and continued registering. He called "Herman". A fat Gestapo came over to the table and was shown the paper. He inspected it and went to the gate where three other Gestapo were standing. All three were observing me while looking at the note. One of them shouted: "Jew, come here!" I walked over. "Where are you from?" they asked. "I am from Svyniukhy," I replied. "How did you get here?" "I came to get coal for my work," I answered. The questioning continued: "Are you a craftsman?" "Yes, a blacksmith and a locksmith." "How long have you been working at your trade?" "Fifteen years." "An expert?" "First class." "Do you have proof that you are not a communist?" "I have only my birth certificate." The questions stopped. They discussed something between them, and the older Gestapo returned the ticket, saying that Jews were working very hard for them. He told me to take the note and go back to work. I left the place.

Back in town, I noticed that things were really simmering. The screaming could be heard from a great distance. Large numbers of beaten Jews were being moved by the militia.

The Germans released me, but what could I do now? Where would I go? I knocked on a door, but the woman refused to let me in. I tried another door where a woman with a bloody nose, also did not want to allow me to enter. I was able to overhear a man in another room saying, "Let the man in." As I came into the house I was followed by women crying, "Dear Jew, do you know where they were taken? What do the Germans do on the grounds?" I told them all I knew, but they did not believe me. We were sitting in the bedroom when the man whispered that he thought the Germans would arrive soon to take them also. He suggested that we hide under the bed. Realizing that it would not help, we remained seated.

Time passed. It was 3:30 PM. Women walked in and out, remarking, "They are catching a lot less." We heard that the militia was robbing every house.

We opened the windows and the doors leading to the back alley so that we would be able to escape in the event the militia came. When a woman shouted: "They are here," we quickly jumped out of the window, but two militiamen were right there. They beat us and checked our pockets while they seized us. Everywhere, women were moaning, whining and crying, "Oh God, when will it come to an end?"

We came to the concentration area. It was quiet. A few hundred people were sitting on the ground, holding their hands around their knees with their heads lowered. The people were surrounded by Germans with machine guns and Ukrainian police. "Here are more *Zhyds* that we found," said the militiaman. When I gave the German my note, he looked it over and screamed, "How did you get here, *Jude?*" Right then fat Herman came by. He handed the paper to someone else, and told me to come with them. The German held the note and did not take his eyes off me. Suddenly, he hit me on the head and I fell. I stood up slowly. He returned the paper and shouted, "Run, you lazy Jew." I left the place, and after a short distance, I sat down, thinking, where do I go? A militiaman told me to leave. I went back into town. Crying women asked me the same questions again.

As I entered the house, my sister-in-law Rachel and the wives of those who were arrested from Svyniukhy came in. Moaning and crying, they told me that the jailed men were taken away early that morning. Fraidel did not leave me alone. "Did you see my Shlomo?" "Did he tell you anything?" she kept asking. I told them that I did not see either one of them. I added that it was difficult to recognize anyone because there were a few hundred men gathered there. They did not believe me. I kept trying to explain that they sat on the ground, hands around their knees and heads down. More people entered with the same questions. I repeated my observations over and over again. Rachel told me that the priest tried to get me released when I was already freed.

The priest informed Rachel that the peasant who brought me over earlier would come to the house, and that I should drive the wagon. He also told her that I should remove the ribbon from my arm that signified I was a Jew. The peasant came. I got into the wagon and we were on our way.

When we arrived at the checkpoint at the mill in Skubelki, a suburb of Horochow, I was immediately recognized as a Jew. The peasant explained that he could not drive the wagon because he was sick, he asked me to drive. In addition, he explained that he saw the Germans allow me to leave town and therefore thought that everything was alright. The militiaman claimed he could not let a Jew out of town. He got onto the wagon and drove us to the Skubelki police. The chief, laughing loudly, said, "You are trying to escape?

Ha, ha, ha." I showed him the German note. He became quite serious, inspected the document very carefully. "Explain it to me," he said, "I do not understand German." I took the document and translated it very scrupulously: "I am asking you to release 100 kilos of coal for Svyniukhy," signed, "Wici Bodj." I explained that Wici Bodj was an official in the Svyniukhy area. Looking straight into my eyes, he said "Go, go straight home."

On our way to Svyniukhy, we passed other peasants who asked the one who traveled with us, "So, did they datch all the *Zhyds*? Their time has finally come!" On the outskirts of Svyniukhy, Jewish women were looking over every newcomer, and recognizing me, they were elated. Everyone asked, "What is happening?" I could not answer. I was preoccupied, thinking, "What will be the end? And where can we hide?"

Yecheskel told me that he saw the priest, who related the events that took place in Horochow. The priest said that he wanted to help Shlomo and Avraham but they had already been moved to another place, and that he wanted to help me but I had already been released. He was one man we could believe.

Moshe Gorenstain, an old and sick man, upon entering Yecheskel's house, turned to me and said, "My dear child, did you happen to see my son Shlomo?" I assured him that Shlomo would return and that he should not worry.

The Horochow catastrophe strengthened the positions of the chief of police and the village mayor. They reminded Yecheskel and Yitzhak Pechornik that the events in other villages did not occur in Svyniukhy because they were our protectors. Two days earlier when they were asked if they needed all the Jews in the local economy, we understood what they were really after. We once again collected some very useful items and presented them to each one individually.

On August 25 the Germans entered the village. The militia summoned Yecheskel. Upon returning, he informed us that they imposed a head tax of 20 rubles on every one to be handed over in two days. The Germans' orders clearly warned that those who did not pay would be handed over to the Germans. Obviously, we could not allow that to happen. We had to collect a total of 7200 rubles. Those who had the money turned it over to Yecheskel for a total of 5400 rubles. The rest was very difficult to raise, but it was finally accomplished.

On August 27 Yecheskel travelled to Horochow to turn over the money to the regional commissioner. When he returned, he reported that the head tax imposed on the surrounding areas was even higher. The consensus was "As long as our safety depended on money, the troublesome problem would be reduced by half."

On August 28, the Ukrainians, with the approval of the Germans decided to replace the *Mogen Dovid* arm patch with two yellow round ones, each 8 centimeters in diameter, one to be worn on the left jacket lapel and the other on the back. How low can they get?

From the time the area was occupied by the Germans, the Ukrainian population came alive. Every German was adored. Every day there were new decrees.

The high holy days were approaching, but we did not know whether we should pray or not. The Germans forbade gatherings of people, claiming they were plotting sabotage. A gathering was defined as a meeting of two or more persons.

We decided to present the issue to the Ukrainian officials. The *Judenrat* met with the commandant and requested that he allow Jews to congregate in homes for prayer. He agreed to permit us to pray in a few homes and, in the event Germans arrived, we would be warned. The high holidays came and we organized *minyonim* (ten or more men) in homes. One *minyan* on one side of the bridge gathered in the house of Yosef Sickular. The second one on the other side met in the house of Shlomo Walter and Zalman Linver near the synagogue. We started services at 4:00 AM, so that we would be finished by 8:00 AM. Some people stood guard. The need to pray was very urgent. The crying of women, children, the old and the rest of the community, is difficult to describe. Every one was thinking and asking, "Will we survive to the next year?" At the end we were blessing and wishing each other survival at least to the next year.

The town experienced major changes. The commandant Oleksander Zawads'kyi and his militia were replaced by Andrii Blecher and a few peasants from other villages as the new corps. Andrii convened the *Judenrat* and declared: "From today on I am the ruler in the village. I know how much you suffered under Zawads'kyi. He took advantage of you and did nothing to help. He betrayed Shlomo Gorenstain, Avraham Schwartz and Hershel Diment to the Horochow police for severe punishment. But this is over. Now, you should know that my militia is barefooted and naked, and that you have to present us with tribute as soon as possible, and then we hope that everything will be allright."

The change in the militia hurt us very badly. We knew that Zawads'kyi was an officer under Petlura, but Andrii had a worse reputation than Zawads'kyi. Once again we started to collect valuables and money and handed them over to the police. Without any consideration for the payoffs, the terror continued. The new militia learned how to use terror very quickly. Rachel Lichter and Devora Groiss were so horribly terrorized, that they were unable to walk.

Every evening a large crowd of young Ukrainians gathered in the club house to amuse themselves by mocking Jews. Daily life was isolated and any news from the outside newspapers was unavailable in the Ukrainian language and no one wanted to read them anyway. They reported only the German victories and made a mockery of the Jews. The interest in culture was extremely low. The feeling was that the newspaper was the symbol of cultural progress in the twentieth century.

The registering of craftsmen and the unskilled was already boring, everyday the same story. The Ukrainians were always trying to weaken and debase the workers.

Working conditions were extremely difficult. More people were demanded, especially servants. With the unrelenting driving rains, many suffered from colds. Medical help was not available. The officials did not care. Their only concern was putting more people to work. The *Judenrat* tried very hard to avoid shedding unnecessary and useless tears. They were trying their best.

The approaching winter caused grave concern. It was painfully obvious we needed food. The top priorities were getting potatoes, wood and bread, which were not readily obtainable. The peasants were afraid to trade with Jews, because it was forbidden. However, they had to sell their produce and they needed many items and services which the Jews could supply, so they had to come to trade with us secretly.

It was raining. We were hoping that it would continue. The heavier the downpour, the better off we were. A rainy day brought less likelihood of being victimized and robbed. We knew that the out-of-town militiamen would not maraud in the rain.

It was October 18, 1941. Notices were posted all over the village demanding that all livestock (goats and cows) be turned over to the German authorities, and that anyone disobeying this order would be executed. This new decree had a terrible impact, because a main nutritional requisite for small children was milk. The village committee notified Yecheskel that all the livestock had to be transferred to Koniuchy. The Jews in the village had 42 animals. Women and children took them to the gathering area. Other Jews from the surrounding territories were bringing their livestock to the prescribed place, as well.

The weather was cold. The terror had abated somewhat. Available food resources were few. We only had some bread and potatoes. The situation was very bad.

In the evenings neighbors would meet to discuss the situation. There was always the same question: "Will the Germans continue to advance as rapidly as they did before? We kept reminding ourselves of Napoleon's victories and his eventual failure in the Russian frigid winter of snow, mud, and starvation. We were confident and comforted by the inevitableness of the German defeat, but would we remain alive to witness it?

THREE
LIFE IN THE LUKACZE GHETTO AND SVYNIUKHY

On an overcast day on November 3, 1941, some of us were sitting together in Yecheskel's house. Outside a wagon stopped. The group ran out through back doors looking for a place to hide. A man covered with multiple layers of clothing entered the house. He removed the fur and commented that the temperature outside was below freezing. Yecheskel offered him a chair and he asked for tea. Yecheskel said, "I think I know you." "Yes," he answered. "Are you coming from Horochow?" "Yes," he said again. "Please, tell us, what is happening there," said Yecheskel. Looking around he asked who I was. Yecheskel explained that I was his brother. The stranger groaned and said, "It's bad, they are erecting a ghetto in Horochow. All the Jews have been ordered to gather in a predetermined location in town tomorrow at 12:00 noon. It is very difficult. Remember, there are no wagons to move things, people are carrying everything on their backs and through the mud. You can hear the crying and moaning from a distance." With the arrival of Motal Wallach, the Christian stopped talking, dressed and left.

Life in the Lukacze Ghetto and Svyniukhy

The news about a ghetto in Horochow spread rapidly in our village. Other gentiles had the same report. People were panicking. We began to worry about the creation of a ghetto in our area, as well.

We went to bed worrying about the expected morning news. From early in the morning people were gathering in Yecheskel's house. Yankel Fichman was posted at the door, watching for the militia. We saw a few militiamen on horses and in wagons. They were followed by two wagons filled with Germans. The crowd spread, everyone keeping their heavy thoughts to themselves. We became paranoid about every move being directed against us.

A militiaman asked Yecheskel to come to him. Every time he was called, we learned to expect new demands. This time we had a vested interest in what was happening, more so than ever before.

When an hour passed and Yecheskel failed to return we sent children to find out what was happening. When Yecheskel finally appeared he was immediately surrounded, although meetings were not permitted. Worried and depressed, he announced the Germans' new decree. By the next morning the village must be cleared of Jews. We are going to be sent to a new ghetto in Lukacze the Germans were establishing. They would supply us with six wagons solely for transferring the children. Yecheskel described his pleading, that with only six wagons it would be impossible to transfer all the children, the old and the sick. He described his begging, and bribing offers to the Germans to allow those who could afford a wagon to be allowed to get one. Finally, they called the district commander in

Horochow, who approved the request, on condition that people take only bedding and blankets. For food, we were allowed only potatoes, no utensils. After an inspection, anyone who disobeyed this order would be severely punished.

The orders broke everyone's morale. After many generations of living in the village, we were forced to leave and move into a ghetto. People were crying, groaning and moaning. Many were confused. Some went to look for wagons to move their possessions. The village was surrounded by police, who were ordered to search every Jew who left to make sure he took nothing with him. The objective was to eliminate the possibility of a Jew giving something to a friendly peasant. While searching my aunt Rachel Zemel, on her way out of the village, they found something insignificant among her belongings. She was severely beaten. There was a rumor that a craftsman would be allowed to remain.

While all of this was happening the day was passing very slowly. Those who returned after searching for wagons said that the peasants were afraid to rent them. Those who were willing to risk it, asked for an impossible payment.

As evening approached, the village was filled with more militia. They were everywhere, carefully scrutinizing everyone's comings and goings. They went from house to house reminding everyone that they had to leave by 10:00 AM. The strict prohibition against taking anything caused us to bury everything we could in basements, bunkers or any other possible hiding place. We were sure that one day we would return to reclaim our belongings.

Life in the Lukacze Ghetto and Svyniukhy 41

By 10:00 AM loaded wagons appeared in the village. The militia and the councilmen inspected everything. The noise and commotion in the streets were incredible, due to the large number of deported and peasant observers descending upon the village from surrounding areas. The peasants, given the slightest opportunity, stole anything they could. It resembled people trying to rescue everything from a burning building before it collapses. Screaming was heard everywhere. Noticing that the operation was progressing too slowly, the militia went from door to door to ask the inhabitants if they had received the order. We were told, "In five minutes you will have to turn over the keys to your house and everything will be confiscated." After that time the keys were taken away, and each house was turned over to a different peasant who was told, "From today on you are the owner of this house and you are responsible for everything in it," as if to imply that the houses would be returned some day. It was already 11:00 AM. In many homes, people were beaten and thrown out.

My father and Avraham Wallach received permission to go to Horochow to learn if craftsmen were allowed to stay. Yitzhak, Wallach and I remained in the village waiting for our fathers.

The Jews left the village. The peasants were robbing the houses, taking anything and everything. One Jewish couple, Laib Kapinski and his wife remained because she unexpectedly took ill, so their stay was extended for two weeks.

My father and Avraham Wallach returned from Horochow and we left Svyniukhy. As we were leaving, the peasants followed us, screaming happily, "We're finished with the Jews." My father and Avraham laughed to themselves because the peasants lost all the craftsmen. They recalled that Horochow suffered the same dire misfortune.

After travailing a few kilometers, we saw a large number of wagons mired in the mud created by the rains. Most people were walking. A loaded wagon was stalled in the Nikito Omanse area. On a quilt on the ground near the wagon were three children, one smaller than the other. The mother was crying. It was Shmuel Weitzman and his wife Chaya (Shmulkas). She was pleading, "Help us put the children back in the wagon." She said that they fell off the wagon when the peasant drove up the hill. All of us picked up the muddy bedding and the children. We placed them back in the wagon. We heard the crying of other youngsters whom we jammed by mistake because we didn't know that they were there.

The road was crammed with Jews and their wagons from the surrounding villages. We walked along the side of the road and discussed the events. It was getting dark when we neared Koslov, the village close to the outskirts of Lukacze. Suddenly, we heard loud crying from Avraham Wallach, who was holding his face and screaming: "Oh, God, where did you take us? Why do you punish us like this?" His screaming epitomized deep emotional pain and the women cried even more bitterly.

It was night when we approached Lukacze. From a distance we could hear the yelling of peasants increasing their horses' paces and shouting obscenities at people. Near the Shainers' house, we asked a few people where we were supposed to go. Everyone was

Life in the Lukacze Ghetto and Svyniukhy 43

rushing; it was impossible to receive an answer. Finally an unfamiliar voice said, "Go to the *Tarbut Shula* (Tarbut School)."

Getting through the mud in a narrow alley was extremely difficult. The wheels sank up to the hubs. We were stuck and could not continue. Mired wagons were lined up, unable to move. Some younger men tried to find out where to go. As we inched forward, the alley narrowed and was jammed with people. Many places were almost impossible to pass through. As we approached the *Tarbut Shula*, the screaming and crying increased in volume. It was terrible. In the *Tarbut Shula* we stepped on clothing, firewood and even people, because the floor was completely occupied by them. Worst of all were the constant cries of children, "Mother, mother, it is cold."

We walked into the school that was illuminated and extremely crowded. One teen-ager was wandering about repeating in Polish: *"Grunt sia nia przejmowac."* (The important thing is not to take it to heart.) We were stunned at what we saw; seeing all the confusion around, we decided to return to the wagons. On the way back Yitzhak Wallach tripped over something, which he discovered was a child, who screamed and cried.

Within a short time, it was our turn in the school. We couldn't find a place to put our things. We noticed a small open window overlooking a basement that was filled with packages. We threw our possessions into the cellar which filled it almost to the ceiling. We got down into this place and fell asleep. A light coming through the small window woke us. We realized that inside the dismal place lying very close to each other families became integrated. The heat was unbearable. People were wet with sweat. Yitzhak Wallach told me, "Come, come, let's go out into the street." It was very difficult to get out. In the morning cold, we were finally able to catch our breath. It was almost a blessing to be outdoors.

Sitting there were the young and the old. The children, covered, were fast asleep. The bundles were next to them in the frozen mud.

People woke from a welcome sleep and began discussing the situation. Yecheskel, Froika Koliner and Shlomo Walter appeared before the Lukacze *Judenrat* to find ways to accommodate us. They returned shortly after. The Lukacze *Judenrat*, Moshe Pechornik and Shainer, told them that there were 1400 Jews in Lukacze and 50% of their houses were confiscated. The rest, occupied by peasants, would be available (hopefully) at any moment. They explained that they could not accommodate our village; their first priority was their own people, they said, "The population in Lukacze was increased by 800 from Svyniukhy and the neighboring area. Right now we are helpless. It will take a few days to find a solution. You are not the only ones in such a situation. Any one who can resolve this predicament with the help of friends or family, should do so." In addition, they told us that in accordance with the commissioner's orders we had to prepare a list of our people by trade: craftsmen and the rest.

The entire day passed in the narrow, noisy, muddy alleys looking for an apartment. Every one was on the lookout for a shelter, anything was acceptable, even the worst; it did not matter. We heard about house-

Life in the Lukacze Ghetto and Svyniukhy 45

holds that made some space available. People moved into rooms without windows or doors, even into stables. Stalls were converted into rooms and were called home. It was impossible to find an apartment in the ghetto. Everyone did the best he or she could.

We started to make furniture in the ghetto. Everywhere people were making tables, beds, benches and stools, to the best of their ability and with regard to their need. Children and women worked with wood, everyone learned to do something.

On November 6, the town council ordered us to submit, by November 8, a list of all those in the ghetto and a census of the craftsmen. Everyone had to be registered. Any one who failed to do so was risking his or her life. All those between the ages of 18 and 55 would be registered on the work list. The town was divided between craftsmen and the unskilled. Craftsmen would not be allowed to live with those who weren't.

It was becoming more difficult to get bread; the shortage was evident. Very few had flour and there were no facilities for baking. On November 7, we were informed about a new decree which would enable everyone to receive bread from their village representatives. At 10:00 AM on the following morning, people were lined up. They all received 140 grams of bread a day and additional portions retroactive for the previous three days. Starting on the following day every family would receive bread coupons. The bread distribution would be administered from the large building near Moshe Pechornik's house. The government price for the bread was 1 ruble per kilo.

The newcomers asked to see the *Judenrat*, to help arrange a meeting with the regional commissioner to plead with him to permit people to return to their homes for furniture, potatoes and wood that might possibly still be there. The *Judenrat* presented the chief of police with a present, to assure that their request would reach headquarters in Horochow. The *Judenrat* requested an audience with the regional commissioner in Horochow.

On November 11, with the approval of the Lukacze police commissioner, the *Judenrat* went to Horochow. Impatiently, we awaited their return. That evening, gathered at Pechornik's, we learned that the regional commissioner had approved our request. The order stipulated that between 11:00 AM on the next day and the evening of the following one, one person from each family in the ghetto could return to his home and take only potatoes, wood and some furniture, and that only if those things were still in the houses. Anyone attempting to take anything else would pay a dear price.

The news was exciting for the ghetto inhabitants. People prepared. The thought that we were going home was in a sense tantamount to feeling that we were reborn. By 8:00 AM the people were ready to go. At 10:00 AM Sianer and Pechornik (the *Judenrat*) returned from their visit with the police commissioner, called the people together and reassured them that they could leave at 11:00 AM. The Ukrainian police approved 300 people. In the various villages the police were notified by phone that people would be returning between that day and 12 noon of the following one. They were told to allow us into our old homes to take the things that were approved.

Life in the Lukacze Ghetto and Svyniukhy 47

Soon, five Ukrainian gendarmes arrived, and we gave them food and drinks, and in a little while they were drunk. They gathered all the people and announced, "We are taking you home. The *Judenrat* informed you about what is permissable. Let's go." We left the ghetto, and after covering some distance, small groups split off going their various ways to their villages. We Svyniukhers were escorted by three policemen. It was a difficult walk. The young people who moved fast frequently stopped to wait for the slower ones. The peasants along the way came out to observe the march and their children followed us. It was 3:30 PM when we arrived in Svyniukhy. We were allowed to fulfill our mission and they warned the peasants not to disturb us, but that they would have the right to inspect our belongings on our way out of town.

The Sviniukhy chief of police said: "You will be permitted into your homes by the new owners. Those who do not cooperate will be severely punished." Our escort militiamen warned us that if by noon of the following day we were not at the gathering point, they would leave without us and the Svyniukhy police will have the right to shoot on the spot.

We separated, each one going to his former home. I entered my house. Everything was as we left it. Strep (the Pole who appropriated my keys), observing us, said, "You cannot imagine the difficulties I have suffered thus far. A number of times I was asked for the keys intending to remove everything. I argued that it was all turned over to me by the regional commissioner and that everything belongs to the mill. In this way I was able to keep the hooligans off my back." My father went from room to room and began to cry. Strep continued, "The day after you left, Germans arrived with machine guns and took all the furniture and other valuables."

Outside, at the houses, the "old" residents were crying and whining. "Why did we come back? The killers have already taken everything!" A few asked if they could take some wood and potatoes from our cellar. We let them take as much as they wanted. In other homes, everything that was not taken was broken or completely destroyed. Books were torn, floors were rpped apart during the search for Jews in hiding, windows and doors were removed in many places. This was a common sight. We entered the synagogue and saw that whatever we had not taken previously was ripped or smashed into small pieces. The *ezrat nashim* (women's section in the synagogue) was destroyed. It was painful to see.

Some Jews went to the town hall to ask for the leftovers of the German robberies. In the town hall they were told that after they left, it was no longer theirs and that any peasant who wanted, could buy the house. About what was left, the man at the hall said: "We put everything into the cooperative store, and you may go there and take anything that belonged to you."

We turned to the peasants to help us take what was left. There was a rumor in town that any peasant who drives a Jew would be beaten by the militia. If a peasant was still willing to do so, his price would be very high. The peasants checked with town officials about whether they were permitted to take the driving job. At night we stayed with a few people. In the morning all the coachmen who agreed to come, gathered, and so did the Jews. A few people found some of their belongings in the cooperative store. Most of what was there was broken. We took wood and potatoes from the houses; not wishing to leave empty-handed. We gathered in the center of town, where the commandant and the police ridiculed us while checking the few wagons very quickly, and we left. We arrived in Lukacze in the evening.

On the outskirts of the ghetto, women and children looked intently at every passing wagon to see if they recognized anyone. The first question invariably always was: "What did you bring?" People asked about the town and the condition of their old home.

Slowly, life in the ghetto was becoming normal, if one can call ghetto life normal. In the ghetto the *Judenrat* continued to register craftsmen and the unskilled. Only 200 craftsmen were registered. In addition, the *Judenrat* selected all those aged 18 to 55 for work. The registrations were submitted to the German chief of police. Town authorities were demanding 150 men daily for various jobs, mostly house service for those in power and their families. People were ready to go. It kept them busy and free from the constant fear for their lives in the depressing ghetto.

On November 14, the German police chief (*Wachmeinster* in German) ordered all craftsmen to assemble in the front row of buildings in the center of town. There, the Germans were planning the workshops. This demand intensified the unavailability of living quarters, because the craftsmen would need more space than was allocated to them initially, and this would therefore leave less for the others. The *Wachmeinster* and his deputy visited the ghetto frequently to observe the progress in the center. The *Judenrat* called their attention to the overcrowding that developed. People were constantly moving, together with their property. The *Judenrat* arranged for the craftsmen to be excused from work to allow them to participate in the transferal of their belongings.

The work followed a plan. The location was divided in two: in-town and out. In-town workers were assigned to the dirty jobs like sweeping, road repair and wood cutting. Out-of-towners were used to load grain products (100 kilo sacks) and wood and doing other tasks related to transportation. This was quite strenuous, requiring physical strength and stamina.

Since the out-of-town work was much more difficult than the local duties, it stirred up a great deal of bitterness among the others whose labors were much more onerous.

At a meeting of the *Judenrat* the question of sharing the load was discussed. The picture was quite clear. The people of Lukacze knew the town and its present governing group. Everyone who had an acquaintance was attempting to work for him. One had to work. The job assignments might be unsafe. One might be seized by the Gestapo. It was better to work for a Christian, where it was sometimes possible to get something to eat or, in bad times, a place to hide if necessary. The *Judenrat* did not have the power to alter the job assignments that people were able to arrange because of acquaintances in the governing body.

All the craftsmen, it seemed, enjoyed privileges in the ghetto. The town leadership ordered all craftsmen to go to work and permitted the peasants to supply jobs for them and pay for them in money only. In addition,

Life in the Lukacze Ghetto and Svyniukhy 51

if any peasant needed a carpenter, tailor or shoemaker in his home, he could take him.

Craftsmen who worked in the ghetto were allowed to accept peasant customers and the peasants were permitted to drive their wagons into the ghetto to accept or return work. In addition, the craftsmen were permitted to leave the ghetto for employment.

The new order was a great help. The ghetto turned around. The peasants started to smuggle flour, potatoes and other food into the ghetto. If the militia caught someone, then there were those with the right connections to ask for help. The influential people could be bribed and matters would be settled. Or a payoff could go directly to the militiamen.

On November 18, Yankel Meizlish was summoned to the town hall, where he was told that six men must be sent to Svyniukhy for various jobs. They were Yankel Meizlish, Eliezer Meizlish, Zishe Shuster, Yecheskel Greenspan, my father and me. The order came from the German regional commissioner of Horochow. We went to Svyniukhy, where the police settled us into our house (Hersh Diment's).

Although smuggling merchandise into the ghetto continued, there were still serious shortages, especially wood for the winter. The *Judenrat* asked the chief of police to permit a daily movement of people to their own homes or those of relatives to pick up some wood and other necessities for survival. The police granted the request.

The *Judenrat* prepared a list, hoping to distribute the permits among the people. Permissions would be valid for 24 hours.

Those who were allowed to leave went directly to

their old homes, but, unfortunately, many people found nothing there. So they called on friendly peasants begging and sometimes receiving a few needed items. A number of people formed a cooperative which rented a wagon and transferred the collective belongings to the ghetto.

A scandal developed in the Ghetto *Judenrat* which involved favoritism in the allocations of permits. The granting of these adversely affected the work assignments and schedules, which in turn, led to arguments and even fights. People just left without notifying anyone.

The six of us from Svyniukhy felt very uncomfortable. Every evening after our labors were through we could barely endure the emptiness we experienced in our old Jewish town. The tears flowed copiously. We could hear only the whisle of the wind as it blew going through the debris of destruction, through the broken banging shutters and doors. We felt very bitter.

There was plenty of work from the peasants. Every time we met them, the usual themes were insults and laughter.

Eliezer Meizlish and I were in Lukacze three to four times a week. We arrived in the ghetto buoyed with a feeling of warmth and spiritual elevation. Upon our return our fellow townsmen asked questions about everything. They could not understand why the gentiles, who, after so many generations of living together peacefully, became such hateful anti-Semites.

On December 15, posters were placed all over the ghetto asking that all the craftsmen register because the authorities were creating a "Craftsman Park". The news did not disturb anyone. Most of these artisans were already registered. It was a slow process because of the relative personal freedom we were enjoying. Those who registered were forced to do so by the sheer necessity for work, and for economic reasons. Altogether 90 men were documented.

The authorities created smaller crafts centers within the "park" as: locksmith, blacksmith, shoemaker, cobbler, knitter, rope maker and wheelwright. Tools were collected or made by the craftsmen, and then work began in the various localities or centers. We were working 10 hours a day. The "park" had a ghetto inspector, Laib Kaizer and a gentile one from town, Prisarznia. The workers were ranked professionally. The highest was paid 4 rubles per hour, the second received 3.40 rubles hourly and the third was paid 1.80 rubles per hour. Fifty percent from the hourly wages was deducted for taxes to the authorities and 10 percent for "Craftsman Park" expenses. The master craftsman assessed the time required to complete a job.

All those registered were given green patches that read in German, *Stats Arbiter* (state worker), to be placed on their left apparel arm sleeve. Without this insignia no one was permitted outside.

From the day we enrolled, the craftsmen bread quotas were increased from 140 grams to 250 grams. The shortage of food products in the ghetto was severe; it affected everyone. The number of permits for leaving the ghetto and for calling on peasants on the farms grew scarcer each day. In addition, the peasants curtailed their support.

In the ghetto we started with some small trade. We received nothing from the cooperative.

The Christian community suffered a shortage chiefly

of clothes and shoes (cloth and leather). The gentiles were coming into the ghetto to buy any cloth items. Very quickly they found the Jews who were able to supply almost everything. All merchandise was tradeable. The Jewish problem was obtaining food products and how to smuggle them into the ghetto. This was the same necessity for Jew or gentile. Anyone caught smuggling was severely punished. Different surreptitious methods were explored. Before we realized it, a new party became involved; the Christians living near the ghetto. These people got the goods from the peasants, waited for the right moment, then smuggled the goods into the ghetto.

Inside this proscribed area there quickly developed a group of traders who bought and sold many items. Goods were changing hands very quickly. Many of the militiamen were bribed by their servants to look the other way when the smuggling was taking place day or night when they were on duty. The clandestine transactions were conducted by a group of 6 or 7 men standing next to each other moving the merchandise by hand rapidly from one to the other. It was all accomplished in seconds.

The small trade improved ghetto life somewhat, but there were people who had nothing to sell! The wealthy in the ghetto were looking for people to undertake their work load for a payment. The price was half a bread (one kilo) for in-town work and one whole bread for out-of-town labor. This provided the poor with opportunities to satisfy their hunger to some degree. This would happen three to four times per week.

The largest shortage was of wood, because it was extremely difficult to smuggle it into the ghetto. This

Life in the Lukacze Ghetto and Svyniukhy 55

lack was noticeable in the majority of homes; despite the crowded conditions, it was severely cold. Adults wore warm clothes. Children, with their swollen hands, were rolled into pillows, blankets and sheets to keep them warm and they looked very scared and glum.

It was clear from the short stint of work in the "craftsman park" that, in spite of the long hours of toil, it would not amount to anything. The 16 rubles a top rank craftsman earned in a day bought very little in the ghetto. A bread was 25 to 30 rubles. The artisans were asking the peasants for a little extra on the side, and many peasants complied. In the "park" it was considered a gift. When inspector Prisarznia uncovered this practice soon after it started, we managed to pay him off with a few suits.

Taking "presents" became a custom that eased things a bit. Any peasant placing a work order first asked for the amount of the "present". "Presents" usually included bread, potatoes, and several other items. This practice tended to shorten the recorded "working hours". When a peasant ordered work he wanted it done on the spot, and for less hours than it actually took. The cost of a job was determined by the number of hours it would take, but the Christian community was short of cash.

General trade outside of the ghetto ceased. The goods the peasants offered for sale had no market. The authorities were making purchases from the peasants at low prices. Peasants were trading in the ghetto mostly by bartering their food products.

Taking risks by ignoring the need for permits to leave the ghetto, people left to relieve their hopeless situation. The militia frequently seized would be escapees and turned them over to the police chief. The *Judenrat* tried everything to gain their release. On December 15, the Svyniukhy police turned over two Jews, Yitzhak Berger and Yitzhak Klein, to the *Wachmeinster* for unlawful flight. We worried about their fate because it was happening too frequently. We feared that they would be shot. The *Judenrat* quickly collected 4000 rubles for the chief of police and we waited impatiently to learn about their fate. Ghetto militiaman Meir Muller informed us that happily the two would be freed after receiving 20 lashes. Within a short time the two were back in the ghetto, elated by their luck.

The six of us in Svyniukhy were already sick of the place. Every night people from the ghetto came by and we let them in. How the militia learned about this was hard to tell, but they insisted on inspections. Under the bed we dug a large bunker and, when we heard a knock on the door, one of us went to answer and the other covered the bunker under the bed. The militiamen examining the room found nothing.

We knew that people needed help and we tried our utmost in their behalf. If one was finally fortunate enough to exchange something, getting it into the ghetto was very difficult. Successful smuggling was possible only in bad weather, with its attendant darkness and strong winds. The peasants who participated in the operation did not want to overload their wagon sled, 200 kilos was the top weight. We started at midnight. Slowly, dressed in white, we would walk next to the sled into the night. One searchingly looked forward and the other covered the rear. The most difficult part of the journey was passing through the villages of Krimish and Koslov. The town's militia were

Life in the Lukacze Ghetto and Svyniukhy

alerted in the night. When we neared the village, the peasant coachman moved a few meters ahead and we trailed behind. We had a signal. If the coachman spotted someone he would scream at the horse three times, "Veio, Veio, Veio". We would then walk close to the houses or trees, and, when the noise became more audible, we froze in our tracks, listening to what was happening, where people were coming from and in what direction they were going. It was much more difficult with the dogs; they react to the freezing weather. The peasant hardly had a reason to fear. In the event of a sled inspection, he could claim he was moving the goods to friends or family. When we approached the village of Koslov, over the high mountain, we had to make an immediate right turn to the river. The bridge over the water meant that we were close to the ghetto which was situated on the banks of the river. Sometimes the militia was there, but not usually. There were times it was not to easy to cross the river. In many places it was covered with snow over a thin layer of ice and any attempt to walk on it could be quite dangerous. We had to pass there with extreme care. After this, we entered the ghetto.

Across from the entrance near Sianers' house, the peasant made a horse-feeding stop. We looked all around, waiting for the right moment and then, given a signal, he quickly slipped inside. Near the first houses in the ghetto we unloaded everything, and once again, after a close inspection of the area, a signal to the peasant indicated that he could leave.

The creation of the "park" eased things. The peasants were free to move in and out of the ghetto. They also took advantage of the situation by bartering.

58 The Lone Survivor

From December 18, entrance to the ghetto was forbidden. All the workshops were moved outside. Only those with a green patch on their arm, the *Judenrat* and the Jewish militia, were allowed to leave the ghetto. The militia and the Germans scrupulously inspected everywhere.

The Germans suddenly issued ration cards in the towns and villages for the right to grind 16 kilos of grain products per person per month in the mill. Other products were distributed by this method as well.

The act adversely affected the ghetto immediately. It was easier to acquire grain than to have it ground. We tried to find ways to do this. We cut out straight strips of wood 10 centimeters wide and 30 centimeters long and rounded them off. In white sheets of metal we bored small holes that resembled a grater and nailed it around the wood. We set a piece of steel into the wood to serve as a handle for turning. On top of this we placed another piece of metal to act as a sifter with small holes on both sides so that when the two round rollers met, it would grind the grain lodged inbetween. We measured to be sure that everything fit together perfectly. It was very difficult to turn the handles and it was no easy task. The "mill" required 3 men to operate. It was slowly grinding 10 kilos of grain in 12 hours. It did not really grind the grain; it actually shredded it into two or three pieces. Then the mangled grain was placed into a sifter and the large pieces were "reground". In the sifter we found pieces of metal that snapped off from the "grinding" process and were mixed with the grain. Most of the holes were bent back. Many of these "mills" were erected in the ghetto. (My father was an expert in their production).

We had to hide the "mills" in the ghetto. Although not everyone wanted to eat bread from this improvised one, many did.

A different problem was getting any kind of shortening or fat. Oil in the ghetto was totally out of the question. All the factories were closed when the Ukrainians took over. The old dealers in oil were trying to find a way to resume production. It was possible to obtain the raw materials from the peasants. Carpenters, therefore, made strong boxes for this purpose and the locksmith made huge screws for the processing. The grinding problem still remained. Again we built "mills", but this time the holes were very small and the grinding was repeated a number of times. It was possible to obtain only a small amount of oil, some 50 percent less, compared to what was taken from the same raw material in normal times.

On December 20, posters ordered Jews to turn over to the *Judenrat* all furs, sweaters, stockings and gloves. Those not in compliance were warned that the punishment was death. It had an enormous impact. It was decreed in the middle of the winter when it was very cold, with no wood or coal available. The *Judenrat*, accompanied by the militia in full force, called at every home to collect the materials.

People in the ghetto demonstrated against the strict handling of the matter by the Jewish militia and the *Judenrat.* We heard such statements as, "You German servants (referring to the *Judenrat*) are responsible for everything. Because of you, we will not survive." The outcry did not resolve anything. People turned in their valuables. Some burned their belongings instead. Others hid things or smuggled them out to friendly peasants. A large quantity of furs already prepared for the making of winter coats was quickly cut into pieces. Many people believed that it would be better to burn the materials than to give them to the German murderers. However, we still had to hand over some things. The alternative was risking the possibility of being searched, which was definitely not in our interest. During an examination, the Germans might find things like grain and the "mills" or they might take whatever they liked. Realizing this, convinced people to part with the demanded items. The screaming and moaning continued for days.

The *Wachmeinster* with some other Germans came to the ghetto to see what was collected. He inspected and counted everything; a total of 280 items. He became very angry and said, "I will personally conduct the searches, and be assured that if I find anything, the guilty one will be beaten to death on the spot". The chief of police's behavior was well-known to us. At each tax collection he reaped the benefits for himself first. He was well acquainted with weaknesses; excessive shouting increased his profits (payoffs) significantly. After they left, whatever we collected in the ghetto, money and other items, were turned over by the *Judenrat* to the *Wachmeinster*. The furs were packed and the police carted them away in two wagons.

The situation in the ghetto was critical. We were living on 140 grams of bread at the most for a day. Some women volunteered to go from house to house to collect from those who had bread and potatoes for the less fortunate ones. This did not resolve the problem.

After December 28, leaving the ghetto became more

Life in the Lukacze Ghetto and Svyniukhy 61

restrictive. Beatings were quite common. The bitterest enemy was the cold, and wood was extremely expensive. Many homes were not heated and we had no warm clothing either. As a result, illnesses spread quickly, colds were quite prevalent, and a new ailment, scabies, were common. Most homes reeked of *Szara Masic* (a healing lotion used for scabies). The small ambulance was not equiped to handle all the patients; it operated daily from 8:00 AM to 12:00 midnight.

There were three doctors in the ghetto, Dr. Shapira, Dr. Szampan and Dr. Torbeezko. They never declined their services but they had no medicines. Since many of the sick required hospitalization, Dr. Szampan asked the police chief to arrange a meeting for him with the Horochow regional commissioner, who approved hospitalizing the critically ill. However, most of these were rejected anyway. The number of deaths increased daily.

Joining the "craftsman park" became a top priority. Many craftsmen applied to inspector Prisarznia for assignments in the "park", but most requests were denied. Bribery negated the rejections, with suits or other materials. It was effective. Laib Kaizer, the inspector, opened an office in the ghetto. Entry into the "park" became a well known game; it did not matter if one was a craftsman; on the day after a payoff, the person seeking entry showed up with the admitting green patch anyway.

This increase in the entries of "craftsman park" resulted in a more rigorous work schedule which depended on the larger number of craftsmen accepting more menial jobs. Most people that were admitted were laborers. We met with Laib Kaizer and his explanation was very simply, "When a person admits to being a craftsman, we accept him, but since you complain, from now you will have to approve of the new additions." The factories were visited by many relatives and friends begging the artisans to accept them. We had no choice; we had to agree to utilize many. All wanted to save themselves.

On January 5, 1942, the town authorities summoned the *Judenrat* to a meeting. There, they were told that a new decree ordered the construction of a fence around the ghetto. The erection would start on the following day with 50 men. The *Judenrat* was warned not to ask any questions or to seek favors.

The fencing of the ghetto created a great deal of panic. "What do they want to do with us now?" people asked. Assigning 50 men caused problems in the work schedules. The working conditions in general were unpleasant. The frigid weather, without the warm clothes which were taken away, caused fevers every day among the populace. In-town, work conditions worsened because of the inclement weather. Out-of-town workers were replaced routinely, due to the taxing assignments and the daily 14 kilometer walk. The town authorities compiled a list of 2000 and sickness was no valid excuse; everyone had to work. Under these circumstances and in great pain, 50 men were sent for the fencing job.

The physical isolation of the ghetto continued in spite of the difficulties. Since the earth was frozen, steel hooks and axes were used to dig holes. The Ukrainian militia was rushing the workers but it was the weather that actually set the pace.

On January 7, the ghetto underwent a personnel

change. A new German police chief was named. His predecessor was given a 15-day vacation. The new chief summoned the *Judenrat* to a meeting. We were waiting for new decrees. When the *Judenrat* returned, they reported that the new head was interested in life in the ghetto. He asked if there was enough food and wood. After a detailed report, he promised that during his 15 day tenure he would try to help by granting permits, mostly to women, to enable them to go to the villages to bring back anything that might relieve the tenseness of the situation. He also would allow those who had wood outside of the ghetto, to bring it in.

These new tokens of cooperation had an enormous impact on us. We were overjoyed. On the following day 15 women received permission to leave. They went to the villages to collect potatoes and wood. The ghetto revived. Permits to bring in goods were presumably given to the *Judenrat*. While searching an incoming wagon of wood, the militia found 50 kilos of flour. They beat the Jew and brought him to the new chief of police, who asked him, "Who beat you?" The militiaman proudly answered, "I did. I found 50 kilos of flour in his wagon." The chief addressed the militiaman, "After all, you know that I am your superior. You should have brought him to me first, and what to do with him would be my decision." He then asked the Jew, "For what purpose do you need the flour?" "To eat," the Jew replied. The interrogator turned to the militiaman, "Don't you eat? He too must eat," and to the Jew he stated, "Take the flour and go home. Do not trade it." This story engendered great elation in the ghetto. The militia relaxed its stern vigilance, and the fencing of the ghetto stopped as well.

On January 12 an order from the regional commissioner instructed that all Jews working in the villages return to the ghetto. Jewish craftsmen were to work in the Jewish "craftsman park" only. However, the police chief allowed craftsmen to visit remote villages like Svyniukhy, Bluduw and other surrounding towns.

Every day 15 permits were allocated to go to the villages, but instead of 15 men, 25 left. The Ukrainian police did nothing; they knew that the chief would not punish the violators.

On January 16 much turmoil developed in the ghetto; the regional commissioner from Horochow arrived. Everyone knew that his visit meant new decrees. The *Judenrat* was ordered to report to the police chief. People were impatient and curious about the anticipated new orders. After some time the *Judenrat* returned their meeting house. The news was reported quickly: a head tax of 20 rubles. The *Judenrat* was responsible for the payments from all of the ghetto inhabitants. The deadline for this compliance was the 20th of the month.

Money was one of the most difficult things to come by. Sixty percent of the ghetto inhabitants had nothing to contribute. Many suggested that the *Judenrat* should personally collect the money. They arranged a meeting schedule, requesting that one individual from every family visit the *Judenrat* in accordance with the set dates. They asked everyone to help in the collection of the head tax. It was virtually impossible to escape this mandated obligation. Everyone had to pay his share. People argued that although they would like to, they just couldn't. In truth, beside food and wood, they had nothing. How could they comply? The *Juden-*

Life in the Lukacze Ghetto and Svyniuk.

rat cared little about such excuses valid as they might be. They insisted that at least 50 percent of the tax had to be paid, and they refused to argue. They kept calling all of the people for two days and had to do it over and over again to insist that those who did not pay, had two days left.

The *Judenrat* and the militia with an additional 15 Jewish *voile yungen* (muscle men) called on those who had not contributed. The enforcers were divided into three groups. Each one included a member of the *Judenrat*, three militiamen and 5 muscle men. They broke into homes shouting: "Give us the money!" People screamed and cried, asking, "From where?" The militia signaled the muscle men who turned everything over to be searched. All valuables found were confiscated; they also took food and flour. There was great turmoil. The screaming could be heard from a distance. The militia and muscle men cursed vehemently.

Everyone was very angry at the way the *Judenrat* handled the situation. They were very bitter but the money had to be turned over. After the turmoil, the *Judenrat* announced that all confiscated goods would be returned. Claimants were directed to apply to the *Judenrat* for them. A few were notified that they would not get their possessions back.

On January 21, the *Wachmeinster* was back from vacation, which made everyone feel quite sad. The few days of respite with the interim chief of police left their mark on the ghetto.

On January 22, the *Judenrat* met with the town council, who informed them that the fencing of the ghetto must continue. Shainer and Moshe Pechornik pleaded the police chief to intervene and stop the erection of the fence for a time. He explained, "The ghetto was supposed to have completed this job some time ago. Tomorrow the work must be resumed at full speed. The order comes from above." At the same time the *Judenrat* asked for permits to go to the village; he categorically rejected their request. He claimed that he had just returned from Germany and that we in the ghetto were eating more bread than the Germans in their own country. His attitude and behavior earned him the reputation of being one of the worst killers in the ghetto. His attitude was most distressing.

The change in our fortunes in the ghetto was quite apparent, and the difficulties untenable. The increasing demand for workers, with no consideration of the circumstances, occurred again. The building of the ghetto fence continued apace. The blacksmiths and the locksmiths made all the needed nails and from some unknown source barbed wire was obtained. The structure was 2 meters high, with eight horizontal and a like amount of vertical barbed wires giving it the appearance of a net. All doors and windows facing out of the ghetto were secured from the outside with long nails.

On January 25 a two-horse drawn sled entered the ghetto with two militiamen and two Jews. There was a great deal of noise. Chanina Ochsman was killed. It happened in the Wynice railroad station. Germans were beating the Jews who were loading grain. One chased Chanina with a large stick. She tried to escape a beating, but, while crossing the tracks, she was smashed by the bumpers of the train cars. The Germans did not permit anyone to call a doctor, so she bled to death.

Later they sent the body into the ghetto, with a Ukrainian.

The work conditions worsened continually. Daily requests from the *Judenrat* for an additional 20, 30 or more laborers to report at the work site within half an hour, were common. The militia did not care if they were old, young or even sick. The Ukrainians were only interested in obtaining private servants; the person's physical condition did not matter.

On February 2 there was a great clamor. We did not know the cause. We saw the Germans and the militia chasing and beating the *Judenrat*. Everyone was angry. Laib Kaizer ran from house to house in the ghetto rounding up anyone he could find. He gathered 40 men. Hastily and irately, he said, "The office requested us to send 30 men immediately to Wynice to load grain. Before we were able to gather these people, the Germans and the militia entered the ghetto and seized the *Judenrat*." Two Germans took Moshe Pechornik and Shainer, beat them and took them to the police station. There the chief said, "Tomorrow I will ask the gestapo from Horochow to come here. They will show you what it means not to go to report for work." The 40 men were taken away to the Winice station.

In the ghetto we awaited for the return of the *Judenrat*. It was midnight. Full of doubt and fear, we contemplated what the following day would bring. Meir Maller, the first to return, said, "We are free already. The rest of the *Judenrat* is on its way, moving rather slowly."

The *Judenrat* met to discuss the best way to end the episode. First thing in the morning, Laib Kaizer and Shainer called on the police chief bearing a few nice gifts (whatever we were able to find in the ghetto). The people awaited their return impatiently. When Laib Kaizer arrived he declared, "For now, everything is in order."

Trading in the ghetto was becoming increasingly difficult with each passing day. The difficulties arose from the chief of police's return and the barbed wire fence that was slowly strangling the ghetto. Obtaining flour from the outside was out of the question. A small industry developed. Inhabitants in many homes earned an income by providing a service for which fees were established: the price for milling rye was 3 rubles a kilo, wheat 4 rubles a kilo, and cereal (*Kasha*) 2 rubles a kilo and for making oil the charge was 30 percent of the finished product. The "mills" were different. They were improved with new and sample models as well. They were set in horizontal or vertical positions. The majority of "mill" operators were women and children 6 and 7 years old. Two or three children working together turned the "mill". For 20 kilos of grain, they had to work for 10 hours. It was very difficult. A kilo of flour cost 30 rubles and a kilo of bran was 10. Bread made from bran was quite bad; after baking, it would fall apart. But it did not matter, the question was, where do we get even this? We were too hungry to worry about its fragility. The winds outside were getting colder. There were no utensils available for cooking or baking. Having the necessary equipment did not mean that we had anything to cook or bake.

In the ghetto we were faced with the new problem of thefts, which were reported daily. The militia searched homes, but were not able to recover anything.

People were using the synagogues for living quarters

and were burning floor boards for firewood. Tables and chairs were used previously. Old dilapidated homes during the night would lose another part.

The prohibition of leaving the ghetto severely disturbed the life there. The *Judenrat* once again turned to the police chief. Every day he would allow 15 women to leave under the watchful eyes of the Ukrainian militia. These passes caused disagreements among the people, because they all wanted to go. They were permitted to buy only potatoes and oil.

The peasants who were entrusted with the safe-keeping of merchandise and "presents" left by the Jews for smuggling into the ghetto at a prescribed time, resulted in the expropriation of items for themselves or for trading purposes. They were keenly aware of the situation in the ghetto and wanted to take advantage of it. We had to smuggle products and "presents" into the ghetto. The "parks" played an important role in this venture. Every craftsman center created a bunker for their "gifts". Getting them into the ghetto was very difficult, but through police acquaintances and bribery, some merchandise did come in. The "presents" were then traded with the peasants.

On February 15 the *Judenrat* received an order to hand over to the Germans, 60 pairs of boots by the 18th of that month. The news spread quickly. The *Judenrat* held a meeting to determine how to get the boots. It was a major problem. Soon the mud would start to appear. People were rushed to work daily and boots were required. Many did not own these. The fortunate ones would starve before giving up their boots. Many came with a suggestion: if 60 men were forced to relinquish their boots, the rest would suffer as well.

Therefore, it would certainly be reasonable for the collective to help those whose boots were appropriated. In spite of the attempt to handle this situation fairly, those who had to give up these needed possessions did not agree, and acrimonious shouting matches ensued. The argument was logical but theoretical. We had to go to work, but we could not do so, barefooted. Disregarding everything, 60 pairs of boots were seized. On the 17th the police chief came to the *Judenrat*, inspected the boots and said, "Bring them over tomorrow at 8:00 AM."

On February 21, the town council announced that the workers in the "parks" would receive 3.5 kilos of cereal and in the future we would get only 80 grams of cereal a day, and margarine and cigarettes only when available.

All the trade in the ghetto was transacted in the "craftsman parks". Everything that came in passed through the various centers. The workers there played a major role in the ghetto because of their mobility and contacts in the Christian community. Attempts to join a craftsman center were very insistant. It was evident to Prisarznia and even more so to Laib Kaizer. They knew how to take advantage of the situation. Many people could not be admitted because there was an unemployment situation, but the inspectors did not care. If the price was right, there was room.

Mostly wealthy people, not craftsmen, were sent into the "craftsmen parks", presumably as stockroom operators, store clerks, work dispatchers and janitors. Their only usefulness was acting as traders for the collective because they had a great deal of free time.

As the fencing of the ghetto continued rapidly, it

Life in the Lukacze Ghetto and Svyniukhy 71

seemed that the difficulties were mounting as well. Things were getting worse daily. The *Judenrat* discussed the deteriorating situation with many people and they decided to raise a few thousand rubles to remain in a safe place, in case of an emergency. Collections were waning in the overtaxed situation we were in, but the *Judenrat* asked that we give the maximum and exhorted everyone to help in whatever manner they could: money, grain, bread and any valuable possessions. All items would be traded for hard cash.

In spite of everyone's hopelessness in the ghetto, there was one fact that should be noted. The ghetto developed into a rumor-mongering community. There were many versions: the Germans lost the war and their forces were already in Bransk, retreating 1000 kilometers; English forces established a foothold in France; and other stories similar to that one. In general this was good; after the difficulties of survival, the spread of rumors, improved the morale of the people and buoyed their confidence and hope. One could hear everywhere, *"di ieshiah kumt"* (the redemption is coming). The word *ieshiah* was known even to infants in their cribs. Any time one heard a story outside, it was bruited about very quickly, especially by women who were running and repeating it to each other. Soon after dreams were born, followed by the prophetic predictors. These were the daily events, new hopes and new dreams. The actual political news was difficult to come by. It was possible to obtain some information from time to time, from the Ukrainian newspapers, but no one wanted to touch them.

It was getting almost impossible to get illumination. The chief of police had cut the electricity to the ghetto and kerosene was not easy to obtain, so many homes remained in the dark.

On March 16 a woman was walking and crying, "Matis was shot. He was shot for leaving the ghetto." Matis's death agitated the ghetto. This was the first time that he ventured outside of the ghetto after the fencing. He knew all the members of the militia. He was one of those who suffered from the very first day of the war. When the big mill burned, his house went up in smoke. His life was saved but he was left with only the shirt on his back. All the peasants around Lukacze knew him, and were aware that he was blind in one eye. Everywhere he went, peasants felt sorry for him gave him bread and potatoes. This was how he provided for his wife and three small children.

Shainer and Moshe Pechornik asked the chief of police for permission to bury Matis in the cemetery. The request was granted on the condition that the body be taken directly to the cemetery and not into the ghetto first. The Jewish militia and a Christian's wagon transported the body to the cemetery. Many people gathered at the gate and along the ghetto fence, and groaning and crying, they escorted him. His wife, however, was not allowed to accompany him.

After the killing of Matis, our new fear of leaving the ghetto resulted in an increase of 50% in produce prices.

The Ukrainian militia was extremely happy after the murder of Matis. Especially with the chief of police awarding the killer, militiaman Pavluck, for his loyalty. This created a great deal of fear since every militiaman would be trying to prove his allegiance in a like manner. Even the craftsmen were scared. The militia guards were visible everywhere in the ghetto. When there were attempts to smuggle anything into the ghetto, the militiamen appeared as if full blown from under the ground.

On March 23, people were whispering. We overheard them mumbling, "Will they shoot him or not?" The story was, that early one morning, Bairel Raizis was caught smuggling 50 kilos of flour into the ghetto, from a peasant who lived just outside of the ghetto fence. He was apprehended by the militia with one foot over the barbed wire. He was hit over the head with a gun while throwing the flour into the ghetto. Bairel pushed the militiaman and dashed into the ghetto, his clothes torn by the barbed wire. This incident was reported to the chief of police who summoned the *Judenrat* immediately, warned them to extradite the person or else he would enter the ghetto, seize 10 men and shoot them. The *Judenrat*, hoping to save Bairel's life, negotiated with the chief all day. When Laib Kaizer returned, people followed him everywhere, asking for the results of the deal. He would only say, "It will be good." Kaiser told Bairel that a good gold watch and quality material for a suit would resolve the problem. Bairel was able to deliver this bribe in a short time. Laib Kaizer asked Bairel to accompany him to the chief, who would administer only 20 lashes. Bairel refused, arguing, "They want to trick me. Once they have me, I will be killed. If they want to eliminate me, let them do it right here while I am with my wife and children." Laib Kaiser argued that there was no reason for him to worry, and that the chief of police had to impress the Ukrainian militiamen by proving to them that a Jew would not go unpunished. Moshe Pechornik repeated Laib's explanation. Bairel changed his mind and decided to take the risk. After a painful farewell to his wife and children, he left. A short time later Bairel and Laib Kaizer returned to the ghetto. This incident and the general situation heightened everyone's fear.

As Passover approached, the shortage of wheat reached dangerous proportions. We organized a committee to collect money for matzohs (unleavened bread). The *Judenrat* also arranged for a few wagonloads of firewood for baking. The committee decided to install a large oven in the synagogue basement. Every woman was required to work 6 hours at baking matzohs. It was soon quite evident that one oven would not be enough to supply the whole ghetto with the unleavened bread. So the baking had to be done at other places as well. The committee made a serious effort to help the poor with matzohs.

The day before Passover the problem of obtaining potatoes and oil arose. Those two items suddenly increased in price. A kilo of potatoes which usually cost 2 rubles was now raised to 4, and a liter of oil which was 200 rubles was now priced at 400-500, not to mention the difficulty in buying them. Many Jews who had hidden potatoes underground were now digging them out. Aware of the shortage, those who had potatoes were taking full advantage of the situation. The speculators were increasing the price by the hour, causing great anger. There were the *voile yungen* who tried to dig out the potatoes and distribute them among the

Life in the Lukacze Ghetto and Svyniukhy 75

poor. The *Judenrat* forbade this, afraid that the Germans would find out.

The first days of Passover were warm. People went outside. The weather improved morale. The *Judenrat* warned against remaining outdoors for fear of assaults. The Jewish militia chased men back into their homes. Against women, children and the old there was very little they could do.

The *Judenrat* kept the bread in the cooperative. Although only three days of Passover had elapsed, households ran out of matzohs. Women were going door to door in the ghetto collecting matzohs and potatoes to relieve the hungry. On the sixth day of the holiday, many were demanding that the *Judenrat* distribute the bread from the cooperative. People were talking very cordially with the *Judenrat* and appealing to their conscience and emotions explaining that since we were in a very difficult period we should not fight among ourselves to maintain the Jewish tradition. On the morning of the eighth day many people were aggressively demanding the immediate distribution of bread. The *Judenrat* promised that they would do so soon. The day was passing. It was already noon, and people were standing in line. Some even stepped out of the queue to try to open the cooperative, but the Jewish militia stopped them. The cooperative was finally opened, and everyone received a bread. The distribution was accomplished quickly.

Prices suddenly soared. The cost of bread, for example, increased from 25 rubles to 50.

During the Passover holiday, smuggling into the ghetto had ceased.

The ghetto was already enclosed with barbed wire. The *Judenrat* office remained outside. A gate was near Moshe Pechornik's home and another one was close to Dr. Shapira's. All the workers in the "craftsman park" and the others were gathered near the gate every morning. At 7:00 AM a siren sounded and everyone left for work. We were not permitted to leave the ghetto after assigned specific hours. This ban also applied to the people who wore green patches. The *Judenrat* and the militia were able to leave the ghetto only when they were asked to.

Due to the curtailment of free movement, trade in the "craftsman park" was virtually non-existent. Many products were accumulated and hidden in the "park" at the various centers, but nothing could be brought into the ghetto. The only possible way was bribing the militia, but that was not always feasible, because they too were scared.

The warm weather brought the *Wachmeinster* out. He walked around the ghetto. During snow, rain or lightning and thunder, the militia was allowing some things to enter the ghetto. The children played a big role in the smuggling operations. They accompanied their parents to the "park"; there they made small packages for them, and after watching the road carefully, they scurried through the barbed wire fence.

On April 16, the *Judenrat* was asked to supply 30 strong men with shovels on the following day. This immediately panicked everyone. Why suddenly with shovels? Every conversation was concerned with the following day and the coming events, trying to determine where they would be sent.

At 5:00 AM the *Wachmeinster*, in Gestapo uniform,

followed by 10 militiamen, took the 30 men. All headed in the direction of Koslov. We were scared; our eyes followed them. They went to a hill near a brick factory. There they stopped. Near the factory, waiting since the previous day, were wagons filled with Gypsies. The peasants had told us all about this in the "park". A short while later we heard the sound of shooting and terrible screaming. We were confused. What was happening there? The screams abated, but the shooting did not stop. Moshe Schwartz came into the ghetto. Frightened, he said, "I came for an additional 10 men who are needed to help bury the slain Gypsies." At noon the entire detail returned, dirty, tearful and very bitter.

The strong men who returned from the carnage told about the 114 Gypsies the Germans rounded up in the villages and brought to the mountainside, promising to provide them with all their needs: food, land and shelter. They were told that they were settling down so that they would no longer need to go begging for food in the villages. The militia described how the Gypsies danced with happiness, singing and playing their violins all through the night, along with their children who were dressed in new clothes.

In the morning when the militia came, all the Gypsies were asleep. They were quickly awakened and asked to line up near the mountain, presumably to be counted. When all of them were standing, the Ukrainian militia's commanding officer ostensibly went to turn the command over to the *Wachmeinster*, but when he walked far enough away, the shooting by the *Wachmeinster* and other hidden militia started. The Gypsies could not escape; they were against the wall. Small children trying to get away, hid under their mothers' dresses and this was how they were killed. Babies were shot by the killers, going from crib to crib. Immediately after the slaughter, the militia ransacked the bodies for valuables. We dug large holes, collected the bodies and threw them into a mass grave. Some were still alive.

The horrifying events and the terrible ordeal of the Gypsies stirred the ghetto into a frenzy of terror.

We were totally helpless in the face of the vital shortages and the rampant hunger. We had to go to work. The town crews were repairing the roads after the ravages of winter. Many people worked barefoot. Often, although they reported for work wearing shoes, some returned unshod because the shoes fell apart in the mud. Serious diseases and epidemics caused by the filth and overcrowding were fairly prevalent.

On April 22, at eight o'clock in the morning the chief of police called the *Judenrat* to a meeting. He told them that by April 25 they were required to organize 523 people for work. We didn't know what the jobs were or where we would go. We became scared. So many people from the ghetto? All were frightened. We were suddenly reminded about all the men from the town and villages that were supposedly sent to work but were really buried in a mass grave near the hospital. Shainer, Pechornik and Laib Kaizer called on the police commissioner. The *Judenrat* checked the census of the ghetto. The people in the "park" were scared. Others looked for ways to get out of town. In the streets one encountered tearful women and children. Confusion reigned, people wanted to know what the end would be.

Pechornik returned in despair. The police chief

Life in the Lukacze Ghetto and Svyniukhy 79

called the regional commissioner, explaining that it was impossible to gather such a large number of people. The "craftsman park" could supply 130 men. Workers for the chief of police and out-of-town peasants totaled another 80. From a total of a little more than the 2000 ghetto inhabitants, including children and the old, it was impossible to fill the order.

The day passed without a satisfactory solution. The regional commissioner did not respond. The *Judenrat* convened a closed meeting together with the Jewish militia, a total of 12 people. At night, they did not sleep. They sat together quietly, heads bowed deep in thought.

It was daylight again. The *Judenrat* went to the chief of police once more. In the meantime residents of the ghetto who were 18 to 50 years of age were told to be ready for the morning of the 25th. At noon the *Judenrat* returned to report that the police chief had received a new required number from the regional commissioner, 322. The chief warned that if they could not supply that number, he would personally select them. The *Judenrat* and the militia met again. The word on the street was that people had better be ready. It was a critical day. As night was approaching, people were preparing flat rolls; bread was impossible to come by. Impatience was growing. People gathered in small groups to discuss the situation and agreed that the *Judenrat* should take at least one person from each family, not an entire family, even if it includes a few adults. The *Judenrat* tried to halt the gatherings. As the time to leave was nearing, the tension grew. Things were unclear, every meeting was a secret one, and conspiracy stirred the people.

At 5:00 AM the militia moved quickly from home to

home silently distributing notification slips. Soon thereafter everyone knew who was called. The notices made it clear that favoritism and not fairness was the determining factor in reaching a decision. The 322 people included mothers, and fathers of 5 children with weak and/or sick mothers or wives, quite often 3 and 4 adults from the same family. Those who had someone serving in the *Judenrat*, police or other official connections were not called upon even if there were 2 or 3 able bodied men in the family.

The *Judenrat* did not dare show its face outside. Screaming, name calling and curses were heard everywhere: "For two days you were fighting with the police chief. You paid him off with one of our best collections which was to be used in case of an emergency. Who did you fight for? Only to save your own souls!" This was the kind of haranguing that was heard. it was impossible to release all the anger that was building up.

It was 7:00 AM and there was no one at the gathering site. The Jewish militia, holding sticks, accompanied by their Ukrainian equivalents, went looking for the people. Walking between the homes the Jewish militiamen would point out a person to the Ukrainians, who seized him. Those who refused to go were beaten. Many hid in various places but the Jewish militia who knew all of those hiding spots, found them and turned them over to the Ukrainians. Loud name-calling and cursing was heard everywhere. In some cases where they could not find the one they were after, they would take anyone in the home they could, like a brother or sister.

People were taken to the cooperative for bread. Each was given a loaf and then taken to a gathering area next to the cooperative.

Life in the Lukacze Ghetto and Svyniukhy

It was 10:00 AM when the *Wachmeinster* and his deputy angrily entered the ghetto. "Why hadn't the people assembled already?" he asked. The *Judenrat* promised that by 11:00 AM all of them would be there. Many ran to the police chief, asking to be excused, pointing to their bare feet and tattered clothes. He directed them to the *Judenrat.*

At 11:00 AM the *Wachmeinster* ordered the group out of the ghetto. He took only 200 people. He said that in a day or two he would ask for the balance. They were then pushed out of the ghetto by the *Judenrat,* with the Jewish and Ukrainian militias refusing to allow the unfortunate ones even to say good-bye to their families. The *Wachmeinster* divided them into two groups of 100 each, then lined them up, three in a row. People changed places between and within the groups and lines to be closer to a brother, sister, relative or friend. The queues were formed quickly. *Wachmeinster,* after making sure that they were straight, walked between the people, examining their clothes, but mostly their shoes. He asked 8 to step out of line, those who were barefoot and scantily clad (5 women and 3 men). After ordering silence the *Wachmeinster* said: "Do not worry. You are going to work for 14 days. You will soon know where. After that you will return home. Ukrainian militiamen will accompany you plus two Jewish ones from the ghetto, Meir Muller and Kesselman. They will take care of you. Anyone attempting to escape will be shot." He ordered the Ukrainians to conduct a count, then screamed, *"Upfurn"* (go, in German). Inhabitants of the ghetto stood around the barbed wire, looking. Some were calling and talking to their children, husbands, wives and friends.

The workers were led in the direction of Wynice.

The remaining families of the 200 were very bitter. In their homes, people did not cook or eat. They did a great deal of thinking. Peasants told us that they saw the people walking in the direction of Ozdziutycze.

On the morning of the 28th the *Judenrat* was told to send furniture for 10 rooms with all the bedding and all the other necessary utensils to the regional commissioner by May 10th. The *Judenrat* started their collection. Some were assigned to bring in their contribution by May 5.

On the night of April 28, a wagon arrived in the ghetto with Ukrainian militiamen and the two Jewish ones who escorted the 200 workers. They woke the *Judenrat* and told them that by the morning they had to deliver 100 picks and axes for the workers who were selected. The people rose, as from a dream, quite happy. They received regards from the living. The militia collected the materials quickly. Small packages for the workers were prepared. The militia was offered good alcoholic drinks so that they would agree to take the goods.

The stories about the workers were not happy ones. They were housed in a few barns. The nights were cold and their food consisted only of what they got from the ghetto.

Moshe Pechornik returned from the police chief and told us that soon a group of Jews would pass from the Ozdziutycze forests. He did not know where they came from. Many gathered near the barbed wire to watch. Shainer asked the police chief for permission to give them some hot soup, but he refused.

At 2:00 PM, from a distance, we saw a small group of people coming from the direction of Siviukhy. They

Life in the Lukacze Ghetto and Svyniukhy 83

were getting closer. The number of people congregating near the barbed wire, increased. As they approached, we heard names of brothers and sisters who were in the Lukacze ghetto called. Through all the noise we were able to hear that they were from Beresteczko (Berestechko), a total of 200, and that another 100 of them were left in Horochow. They asked that we notify Beresteczko that they were alive and were taken to the Ozdziutycze forest. They told us that behind them was still another group of 140 Jews from Droskapole. After a short time yet another group came. Everything was repeated. We hired a gentile to travel to all the villages to inform them of what we were requested to do.

The peasants who entered the "craftsman park" brought notes from the 200 workers. The hunger was severe; 250 grams of bread was too little to sustain them at work. The jobs were different; some were planting trees, others were cutting them down and some were uprooting trees. The Ukrainian militia was goading the workers, constantly urging them to work faster.

In the ghetto Yankel Blinder organized help for those who were unable to work. He was helped by a few others. The first objective was to collect the 80 grams of grits which was given to the "craftsman park" toilers. A rumor spread that from May 5 on everyone would receive grits. If so, the cooperative would not be the distributor. A discussion would determine who should receive them, the first priority being the poorest. The rest would go to the work camp out of the ghetto. This was not only difficult for Lukacze, which had 600 people in the area. The problem was the few thousand Jews from the farther areas like Lutsk and Ludmir who were living under the same conditions in the work camps, and who needed help. All the letters stressed their dire need for assistance.

Wagonloads of bread, driven by militiamen, were making deliveries twice a week, from the ghetto to the 200 workers. The police chief allowed small packages from home to be placed in the wagons for the workers. In spite of the shortages in the ghetto, every week a few hundred kilos of bread, potatoes and a few other necessities were sent to the 200 workers in the work camp.

On May 5, in the afternoon there was a request for another 35 more workers. The *Judenrat* sent notices to those who did not serve the last time. Again, a stir and arguments ensued, but, with the forcefulness of the Ukrainian militia, the quota was fulfilled. The police chief asked the *Judenrat* to bring those who did not want to go to him. Three people were turned over, Moshe Appelboim, Bairel Shainboim and Meir Diment (my brother). The chief ordered that each receive 15 lashes, which sentence he carried out. Then he demanded that all the 35 be brought there. Shalom Granyc promised to produce everyone in a half an hour, and he did, then two militiamen led the group of 35 to Wynice to work.

On May 7, the police chief notified Shainer that by the next evening all the workers from the "craftsman park" would move to a special division and that the park would be closed. Everything had to be moved. Getting from one place to another created difficulties because there were only a few men available, so women and children had to transfer everything by hand. Changes of living locations ended in quarrels, but com-

Life in the Lukacze Ghetto and Svyniukhy

plications were settled in the end. The Germans observed everything to learn who still had what, and how people were integrating. The division between craftsman and laborer engendered much bitterness.

It was announced that all who were ordered by the *Judenrat* to surrender their furniture and bedding had to do so by the 10th of the month. Bitter arguments ensued and the collection was continuing at a very slow pace. Forty percent of the inhabitants had no furniture anyhow. There were those who did not even own a pillow; large amounts of bedding had been sold. The *Judenrat* went from home to home to collect the required items. It was not easily accomplished. Each prospect sent the *Judenrat* to someone else. At a meeting they decided that by the following morning they must complete their collection.

The militia and 15 Jewish thugs seized a wagon from a peasant. They were divided into two groups with Moshe Pechornik in one and Shainer in the other. From the militia they took Moshe Kokler in one group and Peniameir Meir in the second. They were turned loose on the ghetto. From each home they took whatever they wanted, no questions asked. Their haul included cabinets, bedding and dishes. Many who objected were beaten mercilessly. The professionals in this kind of thuggery were Moshe Kokler and Peniameir; they were already nicknamed, *Gestapowiec.* In the streets a great deal of screaming and cursing was prevalent. All the confiscated items were loaded and sent to the *Judenrat* house yard. There, carpenters and girls were busy washing, cleaning and rehabilitating all of the merchandise. The *Judenrat* notified the chief of police that everything was ready.

The division of the craftsmen worried the people. There were rumors that the Germans would fence in each craftsman group, and that they would be granted more privileges. The idea was to include more people into the craftsmen division. But many were fearful. What if non-craftsmen were discovered near the home of a craftsman? We heard that single artisans pretended to be married. The story spread quickly and many did the same. Arranging couples took place mostly among relatives. Often the participants knew nothing about each other. In some cases it was accomplished for money.

The *Judenrat* was informed that they could divide all free spaces in the ghetto to create small gardens. This information buoyed spirits somewhat. The problem of finding seeds was resolved by the division workers, who obtained them from the gentiles who ordered the work. The *Judenrat* after inspecting the land decided to allocate 20 square meters to each person. The militia made the division. The shortage of picks and other tools was resolved by the extra efforts of the blacksmiths and locksmiths, who made all of the implements. In many places the land was worked. In that effort, the young and old participated. A popular expression was, "In spite of it all, maybe times will get better."

The situation was worsening. The Ukrainian peasants were psychologically deteriorating, as well. The Germans notified them that from the Lukacze area, 11,000 Ukrainians had to leave for Germany to work. It was the same in other areas. With this event, general trade ceased. The largest number of dealers with the Jews had been young Ukrainians. Now they were all gone. Work in the division was curtailed, as well.

Life in the Lukacze Ghetto and Svyniukhy

The *Judenrat* was notified that on May 15 Reich commissioner General Koch would visit Horochow and Lukacze. The police chief told the *Judenrat* that it was most important that the ghetto be tidy. Many homes had to be painted white on the outside and the ghetto must be cleaned, as well. He ordered us to assign more workers to repair, clean and organize matters. During the Reich commissioner's visit, everyone should remain indoors, with no exceptions for the young or old. In the work centers, everyone should be diligently occupied.

The *Judenrat* mobilized all of its strength and delegated, to everyone in a house or apartment, the responsibility of fulfilling the order. Outside of the ghetto everything was done by decree of the town commission.

We were awaiting the 15th, fearfull of new demands. On the evening of the 14th the chief of police accompanied by two Germans entered the ghetto. They were inspecting everything. They called on the *Judenrat* and repeated the chief's instructions.

The 15th was a nice day. At 6:30 AM all the division and town workers gathered near the gates ready to leave. Everyone looked glumly serious. The siren sounded. The militia opened the gate and each group went on its way. In the division, despite the order not to venture outside, every half hour someone left, presumably to repair something, but we were really trying to learn what was happening in the street.

At noon we returned home. People were asking for any news. Filled with fear and trepidation, we survived the day. That evening the police chief informed the *Judenrat* that the Reich commissioner would probably not visit Lukacze. He was in Horochow and in the area.

The situation in the ghetto was deteriorating in every respect. The demand for workers increased, and it was increasingly more difficult to smuggle anything into the ghetto. The question of whether the increase in the size of the division would help, remained unresolved. We were trying to devise ways to increase the size of the division. We learned that the Reich commissioner approved the increase in the number of work centers and the amount of Jews who should work. According to the Reich commissioner, every Jew had to be productive; otherwise, he had no right to live.

There was an urgent need to get to Cimerman in Horochow. He was a key figure in the Horochow ghetto. The regional commissioner followed his advice more often than that of the Ukrainian leaders. With his help something could be done.

On May 18 in the evening, Fayga Weinstein arrived and confusedly said, "Not far from here someone was shot." Many people left the streets. We went out. On our way, near Pechornik's home we heard someone crying, "Killed, such a young person! Killers!" We walked farther. Not far from the Ukrainian militia, a woman was beating her head with her fists. A few other women standing there, said, "he gave a peasant neighbor a pair of pants and two shirts for 50 kilos of corn. We looked through the window. He had the corn near the wire, when the militiaman caught him. He pleaded with them and offered 1500 rubles plus his last suit. The militiaman turned a deaf ear, and just wanted to shoot him. He hit him with his gun and then killed him." It was a clear night and we could easily see Bairel Soltis' inert body stretched out on the ground.

As soon as dawn broke, the *Judenrat* asked for and

Life in the Lukacze Ghetto and Svyniukhy

received permission to bury Bairel in the cemetery. The case of Bairel encouraged the people to become more daring. "From hunger, we won't die. The fight for life must continue. For everyone who falls, fifty will survive."

We kept in touch with our camp workers outside of the ghetto. Twice a week we received information from them. Their conditions were very poor, especially with regard to food. Working in the forest intensified hunger. In spite of 250 grams of bread and the additional 100 grams, cereal and other items from the ghetto, they were still starving.

On the 19th we were informed that two women were raped. The *Judenrat* sent an investigator.

On May 20, the police chief notified the *Judenrat* that Dr. Torbeezko would move into the ghetto. Jews were forbidden to live outside, with no exception. Only Dr. Shapira, the chief surgeon, was allowed to live in the hospital, which served as his home. He was needed.

The *Judenrat* underwent a major change. Shalom Granyc left and was replaced by Moshe Kokler, the militiaman. The official leadership of the *Judenrat* consisted of two people, Shainer and Moshe Pechornik. The rest were ex-officio members, Shalom Granyc, Laib Kaiser and Kesselman. Shalom Garnish, based on his past record, was one of the most devoted of people, always able to find some solution to a most difficult situation. He was very reliable. For the people his word was sacred. No one knew exactly why Shalom left the *Judenrat*. Behind the scenes the word was that he could not abide Shainer, that they argued all the time. Shalom objected to treating people so brutally. The last straw was the assignment of a large number of people for work. Shalom fought against favoritism. Shainer simply told him, "I want it this way. If you cannot participate, then leave." And so he did.

The chief of police frequently entered the ghetto, usually in the mornings. Walking slowly, he observed everything. He tried to seize old people with beards. He would pick up two or three, march them to the barber and have them shaved. The older folks were afraid to go out.

The *Judenrat* made available a few rooms near the cooperative and set up their office there. Shainer moved into a special house in the workers' quarters. The moving of the *Judenrat* presented difficulties, due to the housing shortage.

People returning to the ghetto from their work camps, stayed there from Saturday to 2:00 PM Sunday.

The information about the rape was accurate. The *Judenrat*, seeking the advice of the work camp militia, decided not to turn to the police chief, fearing the worsening of the situation. The work at the various locations became a little easier. The militia was paid off. Even small trade with the peasants was reinstituted. After work in the camp many went to the peasants and exchanged socks, shirts and other items for food. This helped to assuage the hunger to some degree.

On May 25, Cimerman from Horochow came to the ghetto. The *Judenrat* received him quite well and met with him immediately. Cimerman reported the events in the Horochow ghetto consisting of 2000 Jews. "We were well-organized right from the beginning. Fifty percent of the people registered at work centers. We opened various production centers where people had no idea about craftsmanship, and today there are

Life in the Lukacze Ghetto and Svyniukhy

bountiful results. We manufacture cloth, scarves, wood products, shoes, straw baskets and a variety of other things. Beside this, we too have a craftsman division." The regional commissioner expressed the recognition that the Reich commissioner bestowed on the small ghetto and that he was very happy with the results achieved therein.

On the following day, Cimerman and Laib Kaiser visited the craftsman centers. They inquired about working conditions and tried to determine where it was possible to expand. It was agreed to increase the number of people in all of the craftsman centers and to develop one for the manufacture of wooden shoes and another for soap. Cimerman promised to help with the raw materials.

The police chief knew about Cimerman, who was wearing one ghetto patch in front. Whenever he was stopped by the militia and showed them his papers, they quickly walked away. No one would touch him. In Horochow he lived outside of the ghetto. The regional commissioner frequently visited him. In the Horochow ghetto he set the tone. He was very well-liked by the Jews in the ghetto. He was loyal to everyone, and played no favorites.

After Cimerman left, Laib Kaiser and his alternate Atlas attempted to implement the plan to increase the craftsman division. The chief of police supplied half from each of two houses, for shoe and soap factories. People registered for employment in the new centers. Again, people were admitted by the old methods of bribery and connections. Most of those included children of the *Judenrat* and the militia.

The organizing process was progressing very slowly

because of the shortage of tools. The regional commissioners and the police chief did not wish to be bothered. Implements had to be made by craftsmen in their division. Manufacturing soap posed problems. An expert was needed, but not everyone was willing to assume the responsibility, and pay with his life for failing to show results. The work centers increased their numbers by about 130 to 140.

The workers from the camps came home for Saturday in a large group, almost 50. Although the situation was eased a bit by the homecoming, fear was prevalent, and interaction with the peasants slowed down considerably. A non-local militiaman found a Jew eating a piece of bread in a peasant's home. He asked the Jew who allowed him to eat the bread. When he received no answer, he took the Jew outside and shot him. The Jew, Zelps, came from Horochow.

In the ghetto a new idea was discussed, the development of a general kitchen at the work camps, to eliminate the workers' need to cook for themselves. Perhaps the *Wachmeinster* would permit us to buy potatoes from the peasants. The proposal was submitted to the police chief and was approved by the regional commissioner, who allowed the new development to service 600 people. He also permitted two people to go into the villages to buy potatoes. The two men were elected as purchasers; Yecheskel Greenspan from Lukacze, and from Beresteczko, Meir Greenberg. The police chief allowed them to use money only for their transactions. In the ghetto we made kettles for use in the work camps.

On June 5, the *Judenrat* was ordered to evacuate a large house on the main road. It was to be converted into a government institution. The evacuation was very unpleasant. The building housed 14 families. Its location in the front of the ghetto made it ideal for smuggling. The *Judenrat* moved the families with great difficulty; in some instances 7 to 8 people slept in one room.

From the day the furniture was seized, there was no end to their demands. Everyday it was something else: another bed, more bedding and so forth. In many homes people were already spread out on the floor, and it was a difficult situation to say the least.

On June 15, we were notified that all camp workers were returning to the ghetto on that day. This information spread quickly. We were worried because of its suddenness. At 2:00 PM the group of workers accompanied by the militia arrived in the ghetto together with the 250 Beresteczko and Droskapole workers. The people who returned were panic-stricken, asking, "Why are we going home so instantly? Maybe a new danger awaits us?" Shainer and Pechornik asked the chief of police what was happening. He explained that this order came from the regional commissioner and that was all he knew. He would be transmitting more instructions.

The *Judenrat* asked the Jews from Lukacze to help in the settlement of the Jews from Bersteczko and Droskapole. The process was slow. The panic did not subside. On the 16th the *Judenrat* again called on the police chief, who explained that when the militia arrived, the people would be taken out. It did not ameliorate the situation. People were on guard at all times. When a German car was seen, we looked for places to hide.

The Beresteczko and the Droskapole people bought

life-sustaining merchandise. They were quite surprised. "Is it still possible to buy something?" they asked. They described the situation in their ghetto as much worse.

On June 17, the chief of police informed us that the people from the other towns should be prepared to leave that day. We all gathered in the street, waiting. It was night already and nothing happened.

On June 18, the militia arrived. The people from the other towns asked the police chief to let them stay until the morning. He warned the camp workers that if any goods were found in their possession, they would be shot. The Jews who were about to leave resold the goods they bought. The *Judenrat* asked the police chief to at least permit a few wagons to return to take the people back to alleviate the walk back to their own town, 70 kilometers away, with their belongings.

On June 19, the police chief entered the ghetto with seven militiamen. He ordered the people to line up in threes. Bystanders loaded their possessions onto the wagons. Relatives said their good byes and the Jewish militia chased the bystanders so that the chief would not notice the large crowd. He counted the people and at 11:00 AM the exodus from the ghetto started.

The town authorities arranged to have 250 people at work every day. These were divided into three goups: road repairing, street sweeping, and turf digging. The *Judenrat* registered those who were sent to perform the toughest jobs according to the list. The work, supervised by the peasants, was very difficult and demeaning. Our labor amused the audience that was watching. One example of their mindless pranks was an order for us to pile garbage by hand in one place

Life in the Lukacze Ghetto and Svyniukhy 95

and immediately demanding that we return it to its original place.

The Germans ordered the dismantling of the Jewish homes outside the ghetto. People were asked to demolish two homes a day. The peasants appropriated some wood and the larger share was delivered to the town council. Every day hooligans from the surrounding villages came to this work site and inquired of the supervisors, "So! Where are our two men?" presumably for work. They then took them into an empty home and ordered them to dance, kiss their behinds and do other humiliating things too shameful to describe. A refusal earned a terrible beating. The *Judenrat* told this to the chief of police. He asked the supervisors, "Why are these people being beaten?" They explained, "Jews have to work and they should not make deals. If they leave to speculate, we have the right to kill them on the spot if we wish. We are really demonstrating self-control by not shooting any of them." The police chief called the *Judenrat*, "Until now you were just beaten. Henceforth I am allowing you to be killed. What! You want to speculate?" Anything the *Judenrat* tried to say did not help.

The situation worsened as the Ukrainians became the bosses. More and more Jews returned from work beaten and bleeding. The craftsman centers were visited frequently by the town council president, Yakim. When he entered a center, anyone sitting or talking was immediately beaten with his rubber club. He entered our center while we were eating. "Who is the master craftsman?" he asked. Old Yitzhak Lubyszys stood up. "Who is the deputy?" I went over. He hit me and then Yitzhak over our heads with his club. Yitzhak picked up a large hammer attempting to kill him but the workers restrained him and Yakim left.

In the ghetto we felt a little better. In spite of the hard life, it was safe. The militia and the peasants could not enter. Neither could the Germans without permission from the chief of police. Every day Germans came into the ghetto accompanied by the police chief. They walked around and the people hid in their homes. We were living in panic but we became accustomed to it.

On June 28, a demand was made for 50 people to be sent on the 29th to Dombrowa to clear a field of beets. The *Judenrat* prepared a list of 50 candidates, who did not object to leaving the ghetto for some time. The work was handled by the landowner.

On July 2, the *Judenrat* and the militia convened a closed meeting. It was clear that they were quite worried. It was impossible to learn the reason. At the end of the day people became nervous. When the Jewish militia organized a few *voile yungen*, we knew that something was about to happen. Sleeping through the night was impossible.

At dawn the militia and the thugs divided into two groups and entered the synagogue. They were followed by a number of people. Upsetting anything that got in their way, they were obviously looking for something. They found the small "mills", broke them and seized all of the grain they could find. This action was repeated in every house in the ghetto. The screaming all through the area was loud, "Why are you taking the bread away from us?" In the homes that were not yet searched, people hid everything. The militia continued on their rampage, disregarding the crying and screaming. They showed no mercy. Everything was

Life in the Lukacze Ghetto and Svyniukhy

taken. Every home suffered through the search. It was impossible to hide anything from the Jewish militia; they knew all the possible places and they knew how to search.

There was finally no doubt that the regional commissioner had organized 7 tons of grain to be collected from the Lukacze ghetto. After the operation the total amount of grain collected totaled 1.8 tons. The *Judenrat* notified the police chief that they collected only 1.6 tons. The *Judenrat* asked him, "From what source could Jews get grain?" The chief argued that, "The Jews were farmers. When the ghetto was created, many Jews had already harvested their grain. In spite of the prohibition against moving grain into the ghetto, they did so and it was left there, so the Jews would have the needed grain."

The *Judenrat* gave the police chief a few good gifts and he promised to discuss the matter with the regional commissioner and get back to us on the following day. The militia kept looking for and collecting more grain. The situation in the ghetto became quite desperate. Our bread was taken away and we did not know what the future held in store for us. The *Judenrat* said that they would make an extra effort and perhaps they would succeed with money instead of grain. In the ghetto we waited impatiently for the return of the police chief. At 9:00 PM the *Judenrat* came back from a meeting in a better mood. They were informed that the regional commissioner would accept the 1600 kilos of grain, and, as for the future, they would see. In the morning, led by Yakim, a few peasants on their wagons entered the ghetto and picked up the grain. We were left with 400 kilos. Shainer and Pechornik distributed it to those who had nothing left. Intense hunger gripped the ghetto after the removal of the grain. The "mills" were reactivated but, there was no grist. Trade with people outside of the ghetto was dormant.

On July 6, posters in German and Ukrainian from the regional commissioner were placed in the craftsman centers. They announced that from July 5 on it will be forbidden to present gifts at the work centers. Violators of this edict would be shot. Any Ukrainian disobeying the order would be sent to work in Germany. This aggravated the people and undermined the hopes of the ghetto population. The town council demanded that the craftsmen who were permitted to leave the centers for work not do so any longer during the hours of labor. Those caught conversing with a Christian in the street would be shot summarily. It was apparent to all that life in the ghetto was becoming more difficult, foreboding doom. Other options were nonexistent.

The conditions in the ghetto were quite precarious; terrorism was rampant. Turf digging became one of the most difficult jobs. With the lower half of their bodies in the water the workers dug the turf, then they dried it. Even women worked at the drying process. This assignment required a frequent change of personnel. Obviously, the people were distressed; all talk of a better tomorrow and liberation ceased. Everyone was interested in his own welfare.

The workers in the craftsman centers labored long. There was always work. Ignoring the orders, peasants offered gifts for work accomplished quickly. Events in the ghetto were most disheartening. The militia knew

Life in the Lukacze Ghetto and Svyniukhy

that Jews were not allowed to take anything into the ghetto. Everyone and everything were scrupulously inspected at the entrance to the ghetto. Some hid many things under the winter layers of their garments. When caught the perpetrator was severely beaten. Some militiamen seized the items quietly. Mechel Zemel was apprehended and about to be shot, but he was able to escape by running through the gate into the ghetto.

On July 10, the police chief ordered the fifty workers who demolished the homes, to vandalize the Jewish cemetery. They were told to pull up the tombstones and smash them into small pieces. Dirt was shoveled on the graves and the earth was leveled off. Peasants then carried the fragments to the road where they broke them into smaller pieces for paving a road. The workers were very bitter when they returned. Religious people asked the *Judenrat* not to send them on such a job at the risk of forfeiting their lives. The cemetery disruption was a daily occurrence. We bit our lips and kept quiet. Extreme depression set in. People were ashamed to look at or talk with each other.

On July 12, a proclamation was issued confiscating all rubles and replacing them with Ukrainian money. The money exchange would take place in the town vault. The *Judenrat* announced that they would make complete the transaction for anyone who wished it. Some availed themselves of the *Judenrat*'s offer; others held back, fearing that it was a ruse to deprive them of whatever funds they had. Some exchanged the money with the peasants who came to the centers for craftsman work. The *Judenrat* took the rubles to the town vault. However, after turning it over, they were told that

100   *The Lone Survivor*

their money would be returned after the war. This devastated many people because they lost their last few rubles. All the pleas were in vain.

On July 13, the *Judenrat* was ordered to gather everyone in the field near the burned out synagogue, on the following day. There would be no exceptions, not for young or old or workers from the craftsman centers. People panicked. They said their fond farewells. Mothers kissed their children. No one slept. Everyone was fearful of the next day.

At 6:00 AM everyone came prepared, with small packages of food. The *Judenrat* allowed people to gather as families. At about 8 o'clock the chairman of the town council entered and walked around. The peasants hearing about this congregated on the roof tops and other places to watch what was about to happen in the ghetto. The militia hurried about looking into homes, pulling out Jews. Small children left their parents and returned to their homes to check if the Ukrainians were breaking into them.

The *Judenrat* sent two Jewish militiamen to guard against any robbery. Peniameir jumped on a table and said that he would call all the families in alphabetical order; after a name was called, the family must go to the other side of the field. He shouted loudly.

The *Judenrat* left the ghetto to learn what was happening. They met the police chief and two Germans. The chief told the *Judenrat* to gather all the people outside the ghetto at a designated place to which they moved. There a table and chairs were set up. Ten Ukrainian peasants and the mayor arrived.

The mayor got onto the table and asked for silence and bade us to do exactly as he instructed. "All the craftsmen, gather according to your center. Children, under 14, go home. Women with small children, form a group. People aged 14 to 20, stay together. Form groups by 10-year age intervals, up to 60. Wait for further instructions. The doctors are free to go." We were somewhat relieved that at least they released children and doctors. The mayor continued, "Now, you will register by age. When we call your group you will go to the tables and register. First, the 14 to 20s." The police chief and the mayor went to the group of craftsmen and asked them to send the two oldest men from each center, to open the place and to start working. The chief then walked among the women and children. He sent the women with children under 3 back into the ghetto. The registration questions were: name, family name and year of birth. The registration card for the 14 to 20 group was stamped: turf worker. The 20 to 30s were field workers. The 30 to 40s, forest labor. The rest were sent to other departments. The process was very slow. After all were signed up, the militia took them to the other side of the field. From there the Ukrainian militia escorted the registered into the ghetto. The Ukrainians at the ghetto entrance made certain that only those who were brought by the Ukrainian militia, who were everywhere in town, would enter. Anyone who stepped out of a line was beaten. Only the militia and the center workers were permitted to leave the ghetto. It was now noon; the people had been standing for all that time, so they sat down on the ground.

A small rescue operation was initiated. The center workers, those with the green arm bands, handed them over to the older people in the field. The more daring among them placed the patches on their arm and managed to get into the ghetto. In this way, we saved as many as possible. We were scared because the militia knew many people.

The registration continued. It was 4:00 PM already and only a few old people remained in the field. They were divided among all of the tables and the registration finally came to an end. Carpenters and painters were told that on the following day at 8:00 AM they would go to Horochow.

The *Judenrat* wanted to know if all of the 750 registered had to go, or if maybe some could possibly stay. The craftsman centers were left with only 36 men. The Christians were able to convince those responsible, to leave another three men in the blacksmith and locksmith centers.

Every time the *Judenrat* called on the police chief, they were told that all the lists were in the possession of the regional commissioner and that he could not change anything. The leadership of Prisarznia together with the town and the village population intervened to try to convince the powers that be to leave a large group of craftsmen because they were needed. The *Judenrat*, helpless to free them for work, thought of changing the lists. Since 250 people remained in Lukacze for turf digging, they could include any Jews the *Judenrat* sent. The work inspector agreed to alter the list on condition that the police chief and the regional commissioner not learn about it. The *Judenrat* together with the chairman of the work committee changed the lists. The regional commissioner was only interested in the total number.

The people in the ghetto became very tense because

of the sudden absence of the young people. When it was learned that the lists would be changed, they pleaded with the *Judenrat* to allow at least one member from a family that had already sent 3 or 4 people outside of the ghetto to stay and work in the ghetto area. The *Judenrat* promised nothing.

On July 19, the *Judenrat* was ordered to gather all the people at 6:00 AM on the lot near the burned out synagogue. People prepared small packages of food, which was difficult to get, especially in the light of previous events; people paid anything to get some.

In the morning those assembled were ready with their packets, surrounded by family and others. The place was crowded. Present were the *Judenrat* and the militia. At 6:30 AM the work committee chairman arrived, accompanied by policemen brandishing rubber clubs. Imbued with a feeling of power, the group walked around. They ordered the Jewish militia to provide them with a table. The chairman climbed on the table, raised his stick and demanded silence. He said, "I will call the names of those who will be escorted by the Ukrainian militia to work. Anyone who is not where he is supposed to be will be turned over to the police chief to be shot." They called out the names and they reported to the Ukrainian militia. In this way a group was formed. He continued, "Now that we have finished with one group, I will call the second." They organized four groups; the first numbered 70, the second 30, third and fourth, 50 each, for a total of 200 people.

In the gathering area the reaction was terrible; people were screaming, crying and collapsing. Although doctors were present, they could do very little.

Pledges of support did not help. People were saying, "We will not see each other again." Some walked around trying to rationalize that it was not so bad, that it was not the first time that people were taken to work. However, that too was of no avail. The Ukrainian militia lined up the selected ones and they all slowly left town. No one seemed to know where they were going.

The 200 were taken to the surrounding villages. Every day 250 people from the ghetto left to work in the Lukacze area with the majority, digging turf.

On July 27, we were notified at 7:00 AM that all the registered were to assemble on the field near the synagogue; again, they went through the same routine. This time they picked 100 men. A new order included children aged 10 to 14 for work in town, sweeping and reparing roads. Seventy youngsters were registered. Every day they just took as many as they wanted. The children returned very tired, crying at times from beatings. Severe hunger compounded the bitterness of life. Fear and worry were increasing. The ghetto was quiet; people rarely spoke. Women's pale faces and weariness were quite visible. During the last week many died. The daily demands for furniture, bedding, and other items were filled by the *Judenrat* and two militiamen, who were doing the collecting.

On the afternoon of July 29 we heard that one man was killed. The militia noticed him taking a kilo of potatoes and three cucumbers from a peasant. He was taken to the police chief, who told the militia to take him out to the old Jewish cemetery and shoot him. It was Motel Purim. It did not have an impact on anyone.

In the work centers only 60 men were left. There

Life in the Lukacze Ghetto and Svyniukhy

was a great deal of work but no one was in the mood for it. We did not know why. The peasants were willing to bring anything: butter, alcohol, if only we would work for them. They asked for the reason, but we could not explain. We continued to sit at the tables. The militia was with the workers in the villages. In town, very few were left. It was possible to smuggle items into the ghetto occasionally, but no one felt like doing it. Hunger was rife in the ghetto, but people were suffering and only waiting for the day to pass.

From the peasants and letters we learned that the workers outside of the ghetto were working in the fields. The labor was hard, from 4:00 AM to 10:00 PM, with no respite. They were pushed to do more. They were dirty; they could not wash because there was no time. Wagons brought the sick back into the ghetto, some with swollen legs and wounds all over their bodies. The police chief asked that they be exchanged for others. It was impossible. Instead, older-looking 14-year-old children were sent. The medications we used were very poor; there was nothing that could help us. After a few days of rest they were sent back to work.

Michael Diment
Lea Diment, 1990

Standing from left: Haim Dobrovitzer, Yeshua Dobrovitzer, Motel Wallach, Devora (Maizlish) Levkovich, Michael Diment, Shraga Maizlish, Moshe Fichman, Chava Fichman, Lea Diment, Shmuel (Diment) Yahalom, Avraham Finkel, Zisha Fein (1969)

Batia (Diment) Schuster
Zisha Schuster, 1937

Sitting: Peshi Schwartz of Svyniukhy standing are the children.
Courtesy Harry Zemel

SVYNIUKHY 1988

Monument at Swinicher Cemetery in Baltimore

FOUR
THE SLAUGHTER OF THE LUKACZE GHETTO INHABITANTS

On August 19, 1942, there were rumors spread through the ghetto about something horrible that happened to the Jews in Lutsk. No one knew any of the details. The Lukacze ghetto inhabitants lived in fear. In the work centers we asked the peasants if they had heard anything from Lutsk. It was most difficult to obtain any information.

On August 22, we were informed that Shalom Granyc was shot in Koslov while digging turf, but the information was, as yet, not definite. The news spread fast. Curious to learn the truth, we waited until the evening when the workers returned. Shalom did not come back. He had been digging turf when a new German gestapo, the *Wachmeinster*'s replacement, watched the people work. Shalom was standing up to his knees in the water working when the new man told him to go deeper into the water. Shalom did not hear him immediately, so he was shot on the spot. The gestapo asked three workers to bury him just where he fell.

The death of Shalom Granyc aggravated all of the people. Everywhere they were talking about him: how noble he was, how well he understood the Jewish people, that he refused to serve the German beasts, and did not want to take the responsibility of playing the two-party game with the Germans on one side and the Jews on the other. From the time he left the *Judenrat*, he was not sent to work. But he volunteered for the toughest jobs, like digging the turf. He often said, "I do not want to stand by idly watching. I will share in the suffering and destiny of the Jewish people." The older ones gathered a *minyan* and said an *El Male Rachamim*, accompanied by a great deal of crying.

On August 23, the police chief asked for 35 people to be sent to Cholonow, it was not easy to get more people. From the ghetto we already supplied 400, 250 worked around Lukacze, 60 in Horochow, craftsmen were serving in the work centers, and the rest were taken to other locations. All attempts to intervene were of no avail; the people were ordered to be ready at noon. The *Judenrat* and the militia ran through the ghetto picking up anyone they encountered, and they were finally gathered. The police chief along with a few militiamen entered the ghetto to take the group. Every departure created a great deal of pressure, but this time it was an unusual event. Mothers fell on their children and it was impossible to separate them. One woman, Mala Meizlish, was screaming so loudly that everyone stared at her. They all predicted the same fate, "We will not see each other again."

The events in the Lutsk ghetto gave us no rest. It was the talk of the entire community. The peasants who came to the work centers shook their heads, lamenting, "Very bad, very bad." But no one really knew exactly what happened. We heard all kinds of guesses from the workers. Every day dozens of letters from the area were brought by peasants. All of them told the same story, that what happened in Lutsk was terrible. We panicked, and were unable to eat or sleep. Conversations revolved around the events in Lutsk. We did not know what to think or what position to take.

On August 25, we were informed that something happened in Torezyn (Torchin). We sent a messenger there to find out what occurred, while we waited impatiently. By evening our messenger returned. We asked questions, but he refused to answer. His head was bowed. After our repeated pleading, he started to talk. "I entered the town, but I was refused admittance into the ghetto. I waited until wagons entered. I joined them and entered the ghetto, which was empty as were the homes. The militia and the peasants were removing furniture. The peasants were putting the better items in their own wagons and left the rest in another place. Various household pieces like bedding were also collected in a different area. I inquired, 'Where are the Jews?' A peasant looked at me and said, 'What do you think? They will not be here anymore. The Germans and the militia killed them outside of town. The 300 that remain are working in one section under the watchful eye of the German militia. They are being killed everywhere. Once and for all, we will get rid of them.' In the homes everything was strewn about, broken and stepped upon."

The news about Torezyn spread. Every conversation ended with a list of questions, "Will they kill us too? Is all this possible? Can they murder thousands of people?" The workers in the centers became indifferent about obtaining anything. We debated what position to take. Many thought about running away, but where to? We considered Ludmir, a city in Wolynia of twenty thousand Jews who suffered the least from the German occupation. The regional commissioner helped them a great deal. When all Wolynia consisted of ghettos, he claimed that conditions did not permit the creation of a ghetto in Ludmir in the winter, so everything was postponed until May 15, 1942. When other SS groups came to visit, he refused them entrance into the ghetto, declaring that a contagious disease was rampant and that they should not go in. Smuggling was easy, although some were caught and shot. Ludmir was considered a town that did not suffer much. If Ludmir fell, all hopes would be dashed.

On August 25 at night we were told that Barnholtz arrived from Covel (Kovel). We questioned him about the events that occurred there. Looking around fearfully, while refusing his sister's food, he sat, dirty and kept quiet. His sister cried and begged him to talk. He said, "We were working near Covel when the area was suddenly surrounded by German militia. They loaded us onto trucks, taking us in the direction of Covel. Nearing the town we heard terrible screaming and crying. Shots were heard throughout the area. We jumped off the trucks. Many were shot, others were run down by the trucks. I ran without stopping. I didn't even know if I was wounded. A militiaman stopped me, I gave him 600 rubles and came here." He rose, "I don't want to stay here, I will continue on." His sister, "Where will you go?" "Wherever possible," he answered.

On August 26 workers came from the Saduwer forest to obtain food. Accompanying them was Kos Finkel from Torezyn. They were terribly nervous. "This is it, we will all die." Everyone repeated the same lament. "Already, many Jews who ran away from the slaughter escaped to the forest. They were naked and afraid of us. They ran through the woods. As we approached them, they dashed away. When we came across a group, they screamed in fear, making inhumane noises indistinguishable from that of animals. It was very difficult to allay their fears." Kos Finkel was invited into the house. We wanted to learn exactly what was happening. He continued, "When we heard what occurred in Lutsk on Friday and Saturday, we knew that we were doomed. It was no longer an execution of one or two hundred people. Now, everyone was exterminated. We decided to escape. But as soon as we were ready, we were immediately surrounded. Germans and Ukrainian militiamen entered the ghetto. They shot into the air causing panic. Then they tossed people onto trucks. My brother-in-law and I hid. Late at night we were too scared to stay, so we rushed via back roads into the Saduwer forest. On our third day there, we were told by peasants that in Torezyn posters announced that those who survived could return home. There will not be another slaughter; it was only a one-time occurrence. Already some two hundred people were found hiding in Torezyn and they are only working now. We returned home and already met three hundred people. We registered, and were assigned to the ghetto. On the following day the number increased to three hundred and eighty. On the third day trucks appeared once more. We were gathered in one place and told to undress completely. When we were naked, they beat us, threw us into the trucks and drove us out of town to a large pit. They did not shoot, they hit us

Slaughter of the Ghetto Inhabitants 111

over the head with heavy clubs and threw us into the pit. They beat me on my back with a large stick and I ran again, totally nude. I heard shooting behind me. I finally reached the forest. At night I went to a peasant who gave me a shirt and a pair of pants. The peasant pointed to my bloody wound. This was done by the Ukrainians alone. The Germans had no part in this debacle. In the meantime I am with the Lukacze workers."

On August 28, we sent a messenger to Ludmir to find out what was on the Jews' minds there. He brought back a letter which explained that the Ludmir Jews were living under the same terror. The regional commissioner could make promises but he could not guarantee their fulfillment. Everything was determined by the high ranking officials. He said that if he could, he would try to help.

Messengers from the surrounding villages, Horochow, Beresteczko and Droskapole, came with letters of inquiry, "What do you hear?" and "What do we do?" From Lukacze we sent a messenger to Horochow, to Cimerman, to find out what he would say. On the 21st, he went to the regional commissioner and told him that the people in the ghetto were living in great panic due to the events in the surrounding villages. The regional commissioner explained that he had no guarantee that in his region those things would not happen. He also said that he was sure that it would not be so imminent because all of the people were working in the centers, and in the forest, and harvesting the grain in the fields.

It was apparent that the number of our remaining days were few. In the ghetto we carefully watched the militia and the Germans. The work in the centers was virtually at a standstill. People worked in the centers but one always remained in the ghetto. Workers also walked around in the ghetto carrying their tools, as if they were on their way to work.

On the afternoon of August 30, dressed in a gestapo uniform, the chief of police arrived from Horochow with another police chief. They did not stay long. The Lukacze police chief travelled by motorcycle in the direction of Ludmir. The ghetto was in a panic. We wanted to send a messenger immediately to Ludmir. We were told that he would proceed by bicycle on the following morning. He informed us of his departure when he left. We awaited his return impatiently. He finally got back at noon. But he refused to enter the ghetto and he did not wish to talk. After many requests he agreed, and entered a home in the ghetto. He said, "I will make it brief. I was not able to get into the city. The militia would not allow anyone in. So what can I tell you? They took the Jews out of the ghetto. Many of the dead were draped over the barbed wire surrounding the ghetto. The screaming was terrible; they could be heard for a great distance. I do not know any more." He left.

On September 1, Germans came into town. They took the police chief and drove away. A short time later they returned from taking measurements near the hospital, according to some peasants. The Lukacze mayor was told to have peasants dig long narrow pits. The people in the ghetto knew the hours of life they had left, were few.

The *Judenrat* brought a number of valuables to the police chief. He took everything, and promised that in

Slaughter of the Ghetto Inhabitants 113

this area, for the time being, executions would not take place. Everyone in the ghetto knew that all his talk was meaningless. People said, "Enough with the police chief. Better to burn and destroy everything than to turn it over to the killers."

There were always eight Jews working in the forest preparing wood for the *Judenrat* but, due to the shortage of workers, the *Judenrat* called them back. Now they petitioned the police chief to send them back into the forest, and he did. Many in the ghetto were willing to pay large sums of money for work assignments outside of the ghetto. They pleaded with the town council for the necessary permits, but to no avail.

A peasant brought a letter from Chalopicz addressed to the ghetto in general, "Our beloved parents and friends. We already said our final farewells to you, and we decided to escape into the woods. We will fight for our lives with our last drop of blood, and we will never surrender to the German beasts. Do the same thing. There is nothing more to say." It was signed by all of the people.

The letter had an enormous impact. People were crying. With a great deal of difficulty a permit for 15 workers was granted, to help in Aleksandrowka. The *Judenrat* chose their children and a few others, including Peniameir, to be part of that group.

On September 2, when Yecheskel returned to the ghetto from Saduw, we gathered in the *Tarbut Shula* (school) to learn about the situation in the forest. We wanted to know if we could organize and obtain some arms. Yecheskel listened to every proposal and question. Then he said, "As you know, I am very well acquainted with the forest, and I know the peasants' views as well. To get arms would be difficult. Normal contact with the peasants is impossible. The key point is that the villages are the prime source of anti-Semitism. To live like other Jews in the forest, stealing potatoes from peasants' fields, is not easy. It is already causing a great deal of hatred among the peasants." Everyone listened carefully to Yecheskel's report, and were deeply affected. Even the hope of living in the woods seemed to be hopeless. Yecheskel continued, "Do not blame me. I want to help as you are well aware. We have to be realistic; or, we will disappear. I have children but I am not taking anyone. If I die, for my fourteen-year-old daughter life in the woods would be worse than death. I think that those who are able to escape, should. In life we experience many unforeseen situations. We should not go like sheep to the slaughter. Even if we are doomed, we should fight to the end for the honor of our wives, our children and our people." Yecheskel's words instilled courage, high spirits and strength in us. He bade good-bye to his family and children and returned to Saduw. He advised many others who wanted to join him, not to do so, because his permit was valid only for two. It was safer to escape at night. Gittel Linver joined Yecheskel and they left.

A woman walking in the street was holding a letter and crying, asking, "How can I help?" We read the letter. "Beloved parents. Remember, these are our last hours. We will be slaughtered as we predicted. However, we did not receive an answer from you. Please write telling us what is happening in your ghetto. What are people thinking and doing? We are waiting for the carnage—it can happen at any moment. Advise us, should we organize and try to escape? We await your answer." Signed, "Sara Schwartz."

On September 3, the dentist and his family, disguised in peasants' clothing, were taken out by a Pole, but we did not know their destination. In general, we heard that all the able-bodied escaped. Small groups in the ghetto opted for freedom. It was very difficult to organize because the majority of the younger people were at work. The organizers were Moniek Lotringer (electric engineer), Bracha Shenoil (graduate of medical school) and Bracha Steren. They encouraged everyone to flee into the woods—they believed it was the only route to take. In the forest people would settle down, hide potatoes and other foods and try to obtain arms as well. Many would die, but some might survive.

Lemel Gluzman was sent by the labor department with permits to take care of some matters related to work and then return, but he did not make it. As he left town, and only a short distance from the ghetto, a militiaman shot him. With the permission of the police chief, he was buried in the old, vandalized cemetery.

At noon the *Judenrat* called on the police chief, but no one knew why. Guards stopped them. They said, "We have orders not to allow any Jews to enter."

We did not want to work in the centers. So the militia entered the ghetto workers' homes and severely beat whoever they met. When Zishe Shuster was hit over the head with a rubber truncheon in his house, he seized a piece of iron and hit the militiaman over the head. When a second man entered, he too was bludgeoned. Zishe's mother helped him. The story spread quickly and it encouraged others to protect themselves.

The peasants knew everything that was about to happen; they therefore went to the work centers to claim their items which were left for repair. The street was dark. A number of people tried to get out. At 10 PM the first group headed for the river when they were suddenly shot at. They returned and looked for another way. But each time people approached the fence, beams of light focused on them and made them prime targets for machine gun fire. It was difficult to leave. The ghetto was surrounded. People kept repeating, "We're going to our slaughter."

At 2 AM when I entered my room, I heard someone whining quietly and then crying out in terror; it was Rivka Weinstein. We rose and she collapsed. Dr. Torbeezko helped her. She told us, "The first victim was my husband." She was crying and screaming, "Now my baby. What is the baby's fault? Why should we all be buried alive in a mass grave?" Her mother and father wailed as well. Her father kept kissing her and said soothingly, "We are not the only ones, thousands of innocent souls are leaving this vale of tears at the hands of these murderers."

Dr. Torbeezko came into the room and said, "We are surrounded. This is it. I decided not to try to escape, although a peasant wanted to help me flee. For one thing, if I could be told a minute before my death that my son in Ludmir would survive, it would be much easier for me. And before the shooting, I would like an opportunity to speak for about 10 minutes. I will not hide. I will join the others in their suffering. What should the mothers with small children, who know nothing, do?" We talked all night until dawn.

Slaughter of the Ghetto Inhabitants 117

Outside and inside, people were walking around, in a daze. Bracha Shenoil and Bracha Steren came by. They were very nervous, and talked incessantly. "All this is the fault of the Jews. They brought it on themselves. They like to meet and talk all the time. That is all. When we learn for a fact that our lives are over, first there are meetings and consultations. Now it is too late, we can no longer escape. Five days ago we went to the *Judenrat* and told them that if the police chief finds out, he will expedite our slaughter. Maybe this wouldn't have happened. Look at them—the 'sold souls'. They sent out their children, presumably to work. We decided to leave the ghetto two days ago. So Victor Fared (the new head of the *Judenrat*) came and said that he is in contact with the militia and he knows when the killings will start, and that there is still time. Everyone pretends that he is bright and that he is the only one who understands. Moniek Lotringer is the same as everyone else. His mother holds on to him, to prevent him from escaping. We cannot understand her. Does she want to see him in the grave?"

Three of us, Bracha Shenoil, Moniek and I, went out into the street. We walked around in the ghetto. People were standing about discussing the fact that we were surrounded and that the slayings would take place that day or certainly within the next few days. "Today is Saturday, tomorrow Sunday, maybe they won't come until Monday." Prisarznia arrived in the ghetto with two militiamen. They went to Laib Kaizer's home and demanded the keys to the work centers. People gathered to listen. Laib Kaizer said, "Now I will not go to collect the keys." When Prisarznia and his two cohorts realized the unstable mood in the ghetto, they left. The story that the center workers were not allowed to go to work spread quickly.

Walking in the street we met Ashkanazi and Kurtz. Everywhere the word "slaughter" was constantly repeated. Kurtz, an educated Jew from Austria who had been an officer in World War I, said, "It is difficult to believe that the German people would countenance such a dastardly act. If I lived somewhere else, say the United States, I wouldn't have believed it." He stopped walking and looked around, continuing, "Ho, how terrible it is, people are wandering about, and children running. The ghetto seems so alive. I cannot believe that within a few hours not one of these poor souls will be alive." People were going crazy. They had terrible thoughts. Mothers knew that their children would be taken alive to the killing fields. All this did not adversely affect the innate humanity of the sufferers. Loud screaming curtailed the conversation. It grew louder. We walked in their direction. Near the gate of the ghetto was a large crowd along with the militia. Kurtz shouted, "What, the slaughter is beginning?"

Laborers from the work localities outside the ghetto were surrounded by the militia. They were welcomed by parents, wives and sisters. Those who tried to get closer to them were beaten. The noise increased. Women fainted. It was hard to tell just what was taking place.

Soon the militia commandant permitted the workers to enter the ghetto. As they did so, the crying started. Children fell on their parents, kissing them and crying at the same time. Discussions which were overheard were, "Why didn't you flee into the woods?

You returned to the mass burials. In the ghetto we are awaiting the end of life momentarily. The murderers are expected." Workers said that they were organized to escape. But a small group wanted to return to their beloved families to face their end together. This group declared, "This is not a life. It will be very difficult to live in a world that condones such brutality." The workers described the situation. "In the morning, we lined up as we do every day to receive our assignments. Suddenly, from close by, a large number of militiamen appeared. We were surrounded. We were not permitted to take our packages. They laughed, 'You won't need them anymore.' We were not allowed to utter a word. This is how we were led here. Two are missing; we don't know who they are."

As we were all talking, a rumor spread that Ashkanazi committed suicide. We looked for him where he had been with us a short time ago, but he was not there. We went to his home and found his dead body. His wife and children described what occurred. "We did not suspect anything. He came into the house, then went back outside. We heard a shot from the direction of the latrine. When we got there we saw him propped against the wall, dead."

More turmoil. More people returned from work. Everything was being repeated. People collapsed in the street. Others searched for a doctor. Dr. Torbeezko helped them. But this did not resolve the situation. We looked for Dr. Szampan. We tried every place he might possibly be. His friends told us that he was not in the ghetto, that he escaped that evening. Fainting and hysteria was rife and those who could help, did so. Most were aided by family. One woman from among the Droskapole workers was already dead. More and more workers were brought in from the work places, confused and crying.

Bread and flour distribution ceased. The *Judenrat*, through the barbed wire, turned to the chief of the militia and asked him to contact the police chief about sending bread. They were told, "Jews don't need any more bread."

Armed guards covered every meter throughout the ghetto, including the river and other back paths rarely patrolled by the militia. Every possibility was covered. The day was passing. We were confused and terrified. The older Jews put on their *Talisim* and socks. At 2 PM, people gathered in private homes and in the synagogue. All prayed. The incessant crying was heard from a great distance. The prayers were of the *Yamim Noraim* (Solemn Days). Women were staying at the *Beth Midrash* (institute of Jewish learning) and did not leave. Wailing and prayers of mercy were chanted in everyday language. Small children with dour expressions on their faces stood by their parents. They were five and six years old and knew about the terrible fight, and that in a few hours they would have to leave this world. Many of them asked, "Mama, why will I be shot?" It was hard to describe the terrible feeling. They cried hysterically. The fear of the youngsters at seeing their parents in their misery increased their terrible crying.

The workers from various locations in the forest were returned. From the Saduwer site only 14 men were brought back. Sixteen escaped, and one was shot; we did not know who it was. Additional people would not be brought into the Lukacze ghetto. All those from

Cholonow, Mirkov and Korytnytsia were taken to the Horochow ghetto, making a total of 18, if they hadn't escaped. This was the information we obtained from the carpenters who returned from their jobs for the militia in Svyniukhy.

It was 4 PM already when all the young people were summoned by Moniek Lotringer and Moshe Kolier to gather in the large warehouse of Moshe Kolier. We assembled quickly. The warehouse was full. Moniek opened the meeting. Talking in Polish, he said, "All of you know our situation; how sad it is, so I won't repeat it. In a little while we will all be buried in mass graves, only because we are Jews. Dear brothers and sisters, now we must fight for our lives and revenge our fatal plight at every opportunity. In short, we have to think about what we must do. If we only were in the woods and fields. The enemy knew how to take advantage of us so we would be forced to fight among ourselves. We all harbored antagonisms against each other, a most useful person or anyone else, and we could not reach an understanding. Now we share the same destiny. We have to destroy our enemy right here and now. We will unify our strength and not attempt to anticipate every action of our foe; our experience has taught us that we cannot predict what they will do. They have already confiscated everything that might be useful to us, from the smallest tool like an ax, a pick or an iron bar; everything was seized, and we didn't anticipate that. When the killers arrive, we should not panic, but attack the enemy, with our bare hands if necessary."

Afterwards Moshe Kolier spoke, "I would like to express my opinion. We have to consider the consequences of a struggle with no weapons. If we only had iron bars or axes with which to kill the militia. With their machine guns, they will slaughter all of us. I believe we should organize into small groups and try to escape from the ghetto. Planning to escape in larger numbers at one time could be disastrous. If we are lucky and succeed, we should meet in the Saduwer forest. These woods are connected to others and could take us to safer areas. There we can assemble a few hundred Jews and decide what to do. Those who wish to remain in the ghetto should remember that they will be responsible for burning everything, including houses and the clothes on their backs."

We discussed the two proposals and both seemed acceptable but Moshe's suggestion received the majority support. Moniek Lotringer called the meeting to order and asked for a discussion. Most people were of the opinion that escaping was preferable and that fighting without arms would be fatal. Escaping into the forest might give us an opportunity to secure weapons for self-defense. Organizing the escape was the last strategy to plan. Individuals arranged for their escape by uniting family and friends into a mobile group. Others employed different approaches.

Evening arrived. The ghetto was in a turmoil. Everyone was on full alert. People were talking about escaping. They were dressed in better clothing and carried small packages under their arms. There were varieties of farewell scenes. Wives and children were escorting the would be escapees. The last words in many cases were, "Father in heaven, please let at least one member of each family survive." Young girls escorted the boys hoping this would bring them luck.

At 8 PM people were still talking about their escape, perhaps via the river, maybe through the center by forcing their way. It became apparent to all that by 10 PM it would be impossible to get out, because of the commotion in the streets. Others claimed that there was nowhere to go, because "there is no one to help us. The fates are against us. The possibility of succeeding and surviving is highly unlikely. The Ukrainians are collaborators and they are largely responsible for our ominous predicament. No one would risk his or her life to help save a Jew." Many did not want to lie around in the forest hungry, dirty and diseased. "The Ukrainians will make sure that no Jew survives; otherwise, they would be witnesses to the barbarism of the Ukrainians." The arguments were repeated over and over again, mostly by Moshe Pechornik. Someone asked him, "So, why did your children escape last week?" He immediately regretted his statements and declared, "I am not stopping anyone. You are free to go, as my children did. They decided to escape. I could not ask them to await burial in a mass grave."

Forty people, including wives and children, gathered in the home of Messer. The oven was filled with stone coal and the chimney closed while they were gassed in their sleep. Means for self-destruction could not be found for any price in the ghetto.

Time passed. People, assembled in groups, prepared for the break-out. They went to designated locations. Moniek Lotringer and I tried to find out if anyone had succeeded in escaping. Near the center we saw a few single people near each other. In the moonlight from a distance we saw the militia moving about. Coming closer, we recognized Moshe Kolier's group. He was talking with a militiaman, asking him to let his group of 16 people get through, for which he would give few valuable possessions. The militiaman replied, "Get along with your valuables, I will take them away from you anyway, after your death." This sort of an answer was repeated to other groups. Some met familiar militiamen, who explained that they would have let them through, but, "We are afraid of the neighboring militia. Every few minutes we are patrolled by the *Wachmeinster* (guard) and his deputy. They drive back and forth on their motorcycles. We are forbidden to let anyone out under penalty of death." They said that if an opportunity presented itself they would allow people through.

It was midnight. Groups started to return home. There were many complaints about the militia. Some returned home bitter and broken, saying, "This is it. Our death is imminent. We will be buried in mass graves." Others said, "We must force a break-through. There is no reason to wait. We are doomed in any event. We should strive, even with our bare hands." But when it was time to leave, many just stepped aside. It seemed that no one wanted to be the first casualty, although it was definitely possible for us to force our way out. The reason many hesitated was that they had another option in mind; there was still a chance for survival by hiding in bunkers, which many had prepared, for a few days refuge and then getting out.

Slaughter of the Ghetto Inhabitants 125

"Why should I be slain now?" many asked. This was the plan and the reason for the quiet.

We heard that three escaped, Yankel Lichter, Ashkanazi's son and someone else. They took advantage of a situation where many peasants from the Wynice area were unloading wood boards; during the noise that the activity created, they fled through the barbed wire. People were very envious. Many others attempted to escape at the same place, but they soon returned. It was too late.

People were back at home where it was quiet. Occasionally, two or three people could be seen walking outside. Moniek Lotringer and I visited Bracha. It was impossible to sit. We felt like leaving, as if we were in a rush to go somewhere, but where to? Moniek suggested, "Let's call on Avigdor Ferd. Maybe he got through. He knows many members of the militia. It might still be possible for a group to get through."

We left. The silence outside was broken by the sound of crying emanating from a number of homes. We arrived at Avigdor's; it was very dark. We called, "Avigdor." He recognized our voices and asked us to come in. Our conversation awakened many people we could not see. We followed the sound of Avigdor's voice. Live bodies were strewn all over the ground. We told Avigdor that it was impossible to get closer. He said, "Thank God, there are 40 people spread out here. They are asking me to help them escape. Step on them; they are the same as the earth." Avigdor's words slowed us down and we could not continue. We wanted to go back home. He shouted, "Wait! I am coming out to you." We met in the street, "What is happening? No one left? There is nothing to do or to wait for. The last-minute resort is hiding in bunkers. I am sure that there, they will not be found. If you wish, I will hide you." Moniek explained that the problem was not us. All the hiding only caused trouble. "Let's not be foolish. Can we really believe that all those who find refuge will survive and later escape?"

We returned to the home of Bracha Shenoil. They asked for news from Avigdor. We told them what we knew and explained our view about the situation. Bracha Shenoil started to cry, "I wonder why everything broke down after such a long period of trust and loyalty." She went on, "Everyone is against us. Doesn't the world know about the terrible deeds perpetrated by the German beasts? Even if only one airplane appeared. Then, if they couldn't help us, at least we could be destroyed together with the killers. But, no one is really interested in us. They sit in the cozy coffee shops reading the newspapers with their large headlines, 'Another 100,000 Jews killed.' It is a daily event. Did the conscience of the world also die?" She talked about her personal life. She laid her head across my leg and said quietly, "This is the end. Let's at least enjoy making love." Then Bracha and I did so. Afterward, we talked until the sun rose.

Slowly we returned to our home. The house was empty. People were away visiting friends, children, brothers and sisters. The majority were sitting together. I fell asleep at the table. A sudden noise woke me. I looked outside and saw no one. Then Dr. Torbeezko entered and I asked, "What is new?" He took me outside and across the street to the home of Yoel Weinstein. Women and children were crying and screaming, "Ho, God help us." I asked a woman, "What happened here?" She did not answer. With some trepidation I entered the house. It was filled with people, wearing *Talisim* (prayer shawls), which covered their faces. Crying could be heard from under the prayer shawls. Yoel Shochet frequently sobbed loudly. "Oh, God. First you placed us on earth. You gave us the holy *Torah*. We carried it through all of our exile. Everywhere we travelled we had to devise ways to survive the brutality of our enemies. We did not forget your name in our most difficult times. True, we are guilty and at fault." He picked up the *Torah* and put it down. "Oh, God, think about what you visited upon us. You sent us *Amalek*. He deprived us of our best sons. Wives and children were left without sustenance and support. They survived seven levels of hell and suffered miseries with forbearance. Have you really abandoned us? Won't you recognize us as your children of ageless generations past and save us? Do this for our blessed children, the *neshumalech* (little souls) who enjoyed nothing. Look at the transparent skin of the orphans." The crying was terrible, people were stamping their feet and tearing their clothes into shreds. He went on, "This is it. Almighty God in heaven, you decided your terrible sentence would be to consign our half-dead bodies to unmarked mass graves. Until the very last minute we shall not take your name in vain. *Adonoy natan adonoy lakach* (God giveth and God taketh away). With your name on our lips we shall enter our untimely graves. Gentlemen, *Adonoy echad, ushemo echad* (God is one and his name is one).

The crying and the panic that ensued was hard to comprehend. Children were bawling in the streets.

There was no one to comfort them. Older women urged the young ones, "Cry children, maybe God will pity you." I went back into the house. Dr. Torbeezko looked at me pensively. After a few minutes, he said, "Will there be a human being who will understand this? Who will be affected by what is happening here? No one."

The sun was shining. The terrible tragedy was taking place during the nicest days of the year. The sun warmed everything. The nights were lighter and pleasant. The sky was cloudless. But everything militated against us. Even nature seemed to laugh at us. All this increased our nervousness. "Are we really the worst of criminals?"

I was too impatient to remain in one place, but where to go? In the street, people moved back and forth, shouting in despair, "When will the slaughter start?" Occasionally soothing words ensued, as, "Maybe God will help anyway."

I went to see Moshe Pechornik. A few Jews were gathered at the gate near his home, looking out of the ghetto, pointing to the fully uniformed and equipped fire fighters, who surrounded the ghetto, observing every corner. Peasants with wooden sticks, iron bars and pitchforks, were stationed wherever there was a gap between the militiamen. It did not surprise anyone; it was apparent that they wanted to take advantage of any opportunity that might arise because of human carelessness, anything to achieve their murderous objectives. Near the *Tarbut Shula* I met Kurtz, who asked, "What's new? Did anyone escape?" Unfortunately, it was impossible to do anything; civil methods got no results.

Slaughter of the Ghetto Inhabitants 129

We entered Kurtz's home, which was inside Barenholtz's house. Barenholtz's sister gathered everything in the house and screamed angrily, "We lost everything. At least the killers will not enjoy it. It's no use. They will get drunk on our blood. We should never allow this. We should fight back with knives and stones. They should pay with their blood for ours." They burned everything. Miss Barnholtz brought out a bottle of wine. "For years the wine has aged the very best. We have a few liters. I am going to smash them. I will not leave even the empty bottles. I will give them poison, the killers." Kurtz shouted, "Wait. The minutes of life left are short. Let's drink and say good-bye." Kurtz's words were appropriate. The sister said, "Let's say good-bye while we are still alive." Miss Barnholtz called Shmuel Messer, Batia Zishe and the teacher Barenstain. They quickly gathered near the table. They served the wine and a bit of food. Kurtz poured himself a glass of wine. The room was quiet. "My beloved friends. Every time in our lives when we drank, the toast was to life and health. Today, we cannot drink to these. Not on the last day of our lives. We can only wish for an easy death. Unfortunately, in the 1920's, we were blessed with advanced technology and culture. It was a time when the world started to develop freely for the good of society. A period when the world began to believe in a brighter future. But what happened? The cradle of culture turned vandal in such a manner that the wise thinkers of the world could not have imagined. Leaving this vale, we must remember that there will come a day when the world will take account of the unthinkable crimes, when people were imprisoned in wired enclosures like animals. They will know that infants at their mothers' breast died because of poor nutrition. It will become clear to the world that small pale children ran through the street bemoaning the destiny that brought them into this world. The world will learn that for a few potatoes and three cucumbers a person was shot; his reward for all the years he worked from sunrise to sunset to earn a piece of bread. No, my friends, we are descending into the pits, but our blood will not rest as long as the killers remain unpunished. Unfortunately we lost, but so did they. I remember well, the words of the murderer: 'When we feel that the war is lost, we will repay the enemies, the domestic ones, the Jews.' But that is not all, there will be many others who will pay as well. They are far removed and refuse to help. There will come a day of vengeance and we will pay back all of them because history records the deeds of the human race."

Kurtz's words made a strong impact on the people in the room. Shmuel Messer raised a glass of wine; crying bitterly, he talked about his two sons who were among the first victims. He said, "This catastrophe is from God. The human is not capable of doing this all by himself. For example, last night 40 people gathered in my house to commit suicide by gas, but you are powerless against God. I entered the room at midnight and all the people remained alive, some only with headaches. Small children were not hurt at all. A person has to admit that it was his destiny." Shmuel's words calmed the temporary survivors.

Many went mad. They allowed themselves to be pulled in any direction, toward good or evil. People had different fantasies. It was difficult to become oriented, what with the panic, the tragedy and the confusion. The drinking, crying and the swearing ended. Miss Barnholtz insisted, "Burn everything in sight." At this moment she tore and broke everything. "Let the world come to an end."

Not minding that it was our fourth day without bread, people removed valuables from their hiding places. There was no shortage. Unfortunately, adults could not eat. One thing they wanted most was to smoke; tobacco was now available. It was often impossible to purchase anything in the ghetto, but now everything could be obtained.

Now whatever one wanted was free. Those dressed in rags had access to homes where suits and other items of clothing were available. Merchandise was willingly surrendered, but who wanted it? Those who accepted the largess were planning to escape. They dressed well. In the street we saw torn bits of Russian and Ukrainian money and even some pieces of dollars and pounds.

Many removed the yellow patches. Others did not, arguing that we should not, "Shame on those who made us wear them. We will go with them into our mass graves. The day will come when the world will become sober, although our bones will be decayed, and the world will realize the heavy guilt against us with which they are burdened. Such statements were heard everywhere. Everyone spoke about how they felt from the heart.

I went into the *Tarbut Shula*, which was very crowded. People were coming and going. There was screaming and crying. Anger was the prevalent mood. At the right of the entrance older people were gathered. Three drills were operating, building a double wall of bricks, which extended from the old wall. We collected all the books (*Torah*), in order to keep them together in one place. The work was going very quickly. At the side, near a table, sat two old men poring over a book, illuminated by two burning candles. I left.

The groups outside were still there. The noises grew louder as I got closer to a large group of people. I heard a familiar voice from some distance. It was the teacher Barenstain, she repeated her words over and over again, "No, no, He will not cause our destruction. We have already survived many exiles, and we have remained a nation. Many larger ones have already disappeared but we are still here. There will be Jews who will remain to continue our glorious history. A revival will take place, a day when we will find ourselves in our own land, like most other peoples. Neither communism nor socialism will resolve the Jewish problem; only we alone can do it. We can go into our mass graves with the full belief that after the war, the killers and their servile allies will be vanquished and we will be reborn." Others argued, "Palestine will not resolve our problem; it is too small. Nevertheless, we remain in exile. Only a world revolution can settle the Jewish problem." This kind of discussion was heard all over and the conclusion was always the same. "Killers, scoundrels, outcasts, can they kill so many people?"

Everyone looked around, observing each other. Young people wandered, nervously. In a few hours not one of us would remain. Why? And for what?

It was 10 AM already. In spite of the difficult times, the day began. Moniek, Lotringer and Bracha Shenoil came to see me. We went to the large synagogue. The place was filled with small children. Bracha Shenoil observed them, looked at us and quietly whispered, "Poor souls, in a few hours they will be thrown into graves half alive. Oh, how brutal and insensitive is the world." The screaming of someone unfamiliar suddenly shook us. "We have to flee; there is no choice." Many people quickly ran to him.

A well-dressed man shouted to me, "Mechel, you have to come with us." He repeated it a few times and added a few other cordial words to me. I looked at the man and I was shocked, recalling a terrible tragedy. He wore gold watches and rings on every finger. He screamed, "I will cut the wire or bribe the militia. I will go first." A man like this already had many people's blood on his hands. In the old days, during the Polish regime, he beat children and screamed in Polish, "Jews, go to Palestine." When the Russians came to the Ukraine in 1939, he was the first one to offer his services to the police, but because of his record as a teen-ager, his application was denied, so instead, he became the most nefarious informer in town. He was responsible for the death of many people. His activities inculcated the deepest hatred of Jews among Christians in Svyniukhy. When the Red Army left, he too was gone. The Germans captured him near Kiev. He registered as a Pole, as one who was exiled to Siberia by the Russians. He received a pass bearing a Polish name, but because of his arrant cowardice, he returned to his mother in the ghetto. In Lukacze very few knew that Shlomo Giszes had some back; it had to be handled very quietly. If the Ukrainians learned about it, many in the ghetto would have suffered. Now mothers surrendered jewelry that had been in the family for many generations, to the nation's new alleged "savior".

The difficulty with the inability to leave the ghetto engenered panic and pressure while searching for new hide outs. In the synagogue Eliezer Meizlish and Moshe Kokler gathered food and bedding for 20 people and started to settle in; the accomplishment was brilliant, undetectable. The fear was that the crying of children could expose everything.

It was night. In the street once again people wandered around in small groups carrying packages. Near the home of Moshe Gotman a number of people had gathered. A beautiful lullaby was heard coming from a window. A woman, next to her baby's crib, was rocking her child, and singing the famous lyrics, *"Shloof mein kind, shloof keseyder, vous darfstoo azoy ying aveckgain fin de velt?"* (Sleep my child, sleep calmly, why do you have to leave the world so young?)

The pressure to escape was strong, even more so than previously. This was the last moment. In the ghetto people said that the *Wachmeinster* would remove Nanka, her sister and the German mail manager from the ghetto. The mail manager promised to save Chava Barnholtz, who worked for him as a translator from the German to the Ukrainian languages. We observed every detail regarding those three people very closely. At 9 PM the three women appeared in the street carrying large packages. They were headed in the direction of Shainer's home. People followed them. They stopped. Shortly thereafter, a man appeared outside of the ghetto near Shainer's place. He switched a flashlight on and off, picked it up and put it down a number of times. The three women went to the wire and slowly passed through it. He took them with him.

The removal of these three by the *Wachmeinster* made a great impression. It was discussed everywhere. The pressure to get out was very intense. It had been rumored for some time that the police chief would save the three women. Nanka, who had worked for the police chief for quite a while, was responsible for the many favors that benefitted the ghetto.

Walking in the direction of the *Tarbut Shula*, the scene was wild and terribly out of control. Blankets were strewn all over the ground. People, apathetic about everything, were sitting near the sleeping children. Only quiet crying and sobbing broke the silence.

We called on Shmuel Messer. My sister, Batia, asked me, "Why do you roam around so much? Why won't you escape? I will accompany the children into the grave." She said the same thing to her husband, Zishe, and added, "Why? How will you help me by remaining here? Go save yourself before it is too late. Good or bad, there is nothing to lose."

The fact that those three women were able to leave was very helpful. Many groups turned to the militia which became somewhat less rigid. They promised that at the first opportunity in future nights, they would look away and allow people to pass through.

Midnight was fast approaching. We were told about a few who got out. We heard a great deal of shooting throughout the ghetto. We did not know if those people were killed or if, in fact, they escaped.

It was daytime already, Tuesday, September 7, 1942. All valuables were destroyed; beds, furniture and other possessions were burned. Holes damaged the pots and pans. Some buried their belongings; maybe they would survive and be able to retrieve their things. The smoke rising from the chimneys came from burning clothes and could be seen from a distance.

It was much quieter during the last minutes of life. The public's morale had totally disintegrated. The killers were expert in all the methods of torture. The crying rose in waves. The horrible days of hunger and the sleepless nights together with the knowledge of the tragic future had already broken the spirit of the people. Old Usher Ingber, a man of over seventy who spent all of his life working and studying, talked to God, "God. I believed in you all of my life. We are your children! We have suffered so much for no reason. How can you stand aside and watch men, women and children, your children, half-alive buried in a mass grave? If you really exist, this is the time to act. If you don't intercede, your existence will be forever suspect. (This was added later.)

It was 2 PM already when the militia and the police chief appeared in the ghetto. It caused much turmoil. Some hid in the bunkers. There was panic, "What? Is this the beginning of the slaughter?" Crying filled the air. We did not notice the arrival of additional Germans. The large militia unit brutally gathered all the people near the synagogue without exceptions. The police chief asked, "Why are you burning everything in the ghetto?" He said he would detain the people in that place until the SS arrived. And it was obvious what the SS was sure to do so.

Gathering the people was not easy. They were viciously beaten. The people, ignoring the large number of militiamen, were striking back with whatever they could find. The fight was brutal. A large number of our young people were in hiding, and in the end they triumphed.

The militia was sent to extinguish the homes that were on fire, stealing valuables while they were at it. They gathered some 800 people. The armed militia surrounded us; they carefully watched every move we made. Most of us sat on the ground with our heads bowed.

At 7:30 PM the police chief appeared and told everyone to go home. He warned that if we kept burning our possessions, it would make matters worse. People responded with, "Murderers, what further harm can you do? We will be shot anyway. For every drop of our children's blood you will pay dearly. Jewish blood does not rest and it will never rest until the murderers are destroyed." Unfortunately, there was no one to talk with. A stone could have been removed from the tears and pain of the people who were lost during the time we were in the hands of the killers. The people, tired and broken, went back to their homes, claiming their last night alive.

In the streets once more groups gathered. Zishe came over to me and said, "Come, maybe we can get out." Together we went to the home of Shmuel Messer. Zishe picked up the small package and put it back down, and he asked Batia to come, too. She answered curtly, "I am not leaving the children." A horrible cry was wrenched from his heart. "Come, let's go," he said again. But it was in vain. His mother told her to get out too, but she refused to listen. She explained that she was going to be slaughtered anyway, so the children could go with her. Batia repeated, "I am not leaving the children." Pitiful crying again. Batia said, "My son is 5 years old and my daughter, 9 months. If they are killed, I will have nothing left."

The bidding of good-bye was very difficult. It was repeated nightly. We walked toward the door, but Zishe turned back and tip-toed over to the sleeping children. He started to tear his clothes in anger and in mourning. His mother and Batia led him outside. His sister, Devora, joined us and we all left together.

We walked to Shiya Yosel's home, where many people were gathered. They were saying that it might be possible to get out and head in the direction of Aleksandrowka. Chaim Israel had a plan that might enable 20 people to get out. He started to line up all those who had been agreed upon earlier, but that group was joined by a number of others. Chaim Israel asked a few of the people to step out of the line, but they ignored him. He argued that he had arranged with a militiaman to free 15 people and that he already took 20. He explained that it was impossible to rescue any more much as he would like to, and suggested that they try other ways. Some left the line. Chaim Israel approached a man named Renna and asked him to leave the queue, but he refused. Chaim took him by the hand and urged him to leave, but he received a slap instead. Chaim Israel returned and a fight ensued, which was quickly stopped.

We moved towards the wire, some 40 of us. Chaim Israel gave the militiaman a pair of *chrom* (thin leather) boots and a watch. He agreed to let 15 people out and said that he would shoot any more who tried to leave. Chaim Israel slipped through the wire as did

Slaughter of the Ghetto Inhabitants 139

Shika, when suddenly the *Wachmeinster* arrived on his motorcycle. He beamed a light on the area and started shooting immediately. The people ran. We did not know if Chaim Israel and Shika escaped or if they were shot. After some time, the people gathered again near Shiya Yosel's home. Zishe and Moshe Kolier went to the wire and asked the militiaman to let them through, but, unfortunately, nothing happened.

It was 1 AM already. Many reasoned that, after the change of guards, it might be possible to get through. People, in small and large groups wandered around with one last hope that the militia would relent and allow them to escape. Moshe Kolier came running to Zishe, "It seems to me that we are now getting out."

Eight people were near the wire. They gave the guard a suit and a piece of fur. He told them that he would soon permit them to go through and walked away. When he returned, he told them to leave the area or he would shoot them on the spot. They realized that his promise was a lie. The eight tried another militiaman and offered him a watch and a jacket, the only one owned by one of the men, just to let them out. He agreed to let 8 people go, if the other militiaman agreed. He returned shortly and said, "Yes, give me the watch, but not eight, only two or three". Zishe, Moshe Kolier and Devora approached him; along with Yankel Blinder, his daughter and Shmuel Kolier with his two children.

Devora, Zishe, Moshe Kolier, Shmuel Kolier, his two children and I (Mechel) passed through the wire when the *Wachmeinster* appeared and prolonged shooting began. We started to run, then I fell. The shooting stopped. I crawled on my stomach. I didn't know where

I was. I continued for some distance, listening for any noise. Lying there, I heard a slight cough. I moved closer to the sound. I heard more coughing from the other side as well, only a little louder. Coming closer a voice asked, "Who is there?" "Mechel," I answered. He said, "Shmuel". Again, we slowly crawled in the opposite direction. Quietly we were on our way. Shmuel, the two children and I behind them. After some distance, Shmuel said, "Do you know where they are?"

We started to move faster, worrying about the dawn. We realized we had entered a forest. In a large clearing, we sat down. Shmuel removed his jacket and set the children down to rest. We sat together talking quietly. A terrible sadness and longing overtook us, and we didn't know why. Suddenly, we started to cry uncontrollably. I tried to stop but it was impossible. We fell asleep remembering that now we had to be on guard. This is how the day passed.

We walked to the edge of the woods, taking advantage of the covering half-darkness of the sheltering trees. We looked in the direction of the illuminated houses. We were suffering from hunger. It was too early to ask for bread from the peasants. Suddenly, we heard a whistle. It immediately alerted us. In the quiet of the night we heard light steps approach. Shmuel shouted, "Jews?" No answer. It grew very quiet again. After a few seconds the soft steps were heard once more. Shmuel shouted as before, "Jews?" At once we heard, "Who is there?" We answered, "Jews from Lukacze". We moved closer. It was Chaim Pechornik, his wife, Batia, and her sister, Pearl. We embraced and kissed filled with happiness, and quietly started to cry. "It is all over. We do not have families any longer.

Slaughter of the Ghetto Inhabitants 141

Today, they were all shot. How our hearts are breaking."

They led us to a small fire. Now we could see each other by the light of the flames. Shmuel asked, "Do you have anything to eat?" Batia gave him a piece of a pumpkin and a beet. It was tasty. They asked about many things. Batia served two small pieces of bread to the children and softly cried, "Our family's bread from the ghetto. Today, they are already lying in the ground".

We told them that we would like to rest for a little. Batia and Pearl spread two blankets on the ground and we lay down to rest; covering ourselves we fell asleep.

Someone shook me awake. "Come", Shmuel said, "come, let's call on a peasant I know. Maybe we will get some food". He handed me a small pouch and we left.

It was daylight. We went to a small house near the forest. Shmuel knocked on the window. A quiet voice from inside, asked, "Who is there?" Shmuel replied, "Me, Shmuel". The peasant opened the window and asked, "What do you want?" Shmuel answered, "Give me something to eat". Through the window the peasant handed a small bread and a few onions. Shmuel whispered to me, "You ask too, don't be shy". We returned, and filled two bottles of water from the bucket outside and left.

A low voice stopped us, "I would like to tell you something." A tall, young peasant named Stachek came by, looked at us and said, "Come into the forest. Then we will talk." We did so and sat down. He looked around carefully and listened for anyone who might come by. He said, "You know me, Shmuel. I will not turn you in. Yesterday, Wednesday the 8th, there was a terrible slaughter in Lukacze. The Germans shot 1126 from your ghetto. The rest hid. Until late night the militia hunted for, and found people who were hiding in various places and killed them. Now the militia is free and will start to search the forests. In my opinion, the place is small. The Aleksandrowka forest does not cover a large area. You will be better off if you move to the Saduwer forest. First, it is very large, and second, you will find many Jews there, so together you will be able to look for a way out to save yourselves."

He left and we started back towards our people. As we passed a garden in the forest we took a large pumpkin with us. Shmuel's children were crying, "Why did it take so much time?" We sat down and discussed all the information that Stachek had given us. We all sat and thought. Shmuel cut the pumpkin and apportioned a small piece to everyone, together with a piece of bread. When breakfast was over, the sun illuminated the density of the woods. All the discussions were about going to Saduw or staying. We decided to enter the forest and look for Jews.

We went quietly, listening to every noise in order to avoid meeting peasants. We moved mostly through the heavy growth of the place. From a distance we noticed that there was some straw on the ground. When we got closer, we noticed that there were people there. We ventured farther, when the sound of voices stopped us. We laid low, and their conversation continued in Ukrainian. We were ready to sneak away, when we heard the name, Zishel. Now we listened even more intently, we also heard the name Vladick, and "Anyhow, he is a good militiaman. In such a difficult situation, he let us through." We were sure they were Jews. Shmuel and I headed in the direction of the voice. We came closer. The conversation stopped. Shmuel suddenly jumped, "Do you see where the Jews are sitting?" We rushed quickly over to the people, while conversing loudly in Yiddish so as not to scare them. They jumped, frightened anyway. A young man started to run. Shmuel shouted, "Bairel, Bairel." Bairel came over, embraced Shmuel and started to kiss him, saying, "Oh, how you scared us."

We all sat down and asked each other many questions, mentioning and remembering our people. After a few moments Shmuel brought all the others together. Bairel told his story. That Saturday at midnight, he, his daughter, his nephew and his brother-in-law's (Fieval's) children were let out by Vladick, the militiaman from Roozistch. He took them through fields of mud. Anyone who didn't have the stamina to carry on, he carried. He gave them food for the journey, too, and he promised further assistance if they were not able to manage in the forest, in which case he invited them to come to him in Roozistch for further help.

Shmuel asked Bairel, "What do we do now? I don't know if you realize it, but now everything is lost. We are without our families." Bairel interrupted with, "I know. We decided that tonight we'd go to Saduw to find a solution. We just have to devise a plan. We are going to have a tough fight for our lives." We sat down on the straw and made ourselves comfortable, relating all the past events and releasing some pressure.

The sky clouded over, followed almost immediately by torrential rains. It grew dark. We were soaked to the bone. After some time the sun shone through and the weather was fine.

Bairel left the forest to gather news. We made a small fire to warm and dry our clothes. We roasted potatoes and had dinner. Two hours passed and Bairel was not back yet. We started to worry. A short time later we heard a whistle, the prearranged signal we had agreed upon. We answered and sat down with Bairel near the fire. He started to tell us, "I met two peasants I knew. They were in Lukacze today. Both told me the same story. In the ghetto, even after all this time, they are still finding hidden Jews. Everyone who is caught is told that he or she would not be killed if they revealed where other Jews could be found and where they buried their valuables. After all of this torture, they are shot. The Jews in the ghetto came from everywhere. The *Tarbut Shula* was filled with loot and so were a few other homes. In Lukacze there were flyers which declared that 'The Jewish race must be totally eliminated regardless of sex. Anyone who hides a Jew will be shot together with all of his family, and his property confiscated. Whoever offers a Jew bread will be punished in a similar manner.' In the meantime the militia is already searching in the villages for Jews."

This information heightened our awareness. Whenever we asked for things from a peasant, it was risky, because he might be working with the militia. Chaim expressed his opinion that we should wait. "There are many Jews who are still in the Aleksandrowka and Wynice forests. We should wait another few days. Through the peasants, we will learn what to do. We should also remember that in the Saduwer forest, we have no acquaintances. We must be careful in everything we do." Shmuel said, "Two days from now might be too late. As long as the militia is not completely finished with the killings in the ghetto, it becomes easier to travel over the difficult roads." Shmuel's words influenced us. After a discussion it was decided that on September 9, we would leave.

We packed everything we had, gathered into small groups and we went, mostly in pairs. Nearing Stachek's house, Shmuel asked him to show us a shortcut through the fields to Saduw. Stachek pointed in the direction we had just exited from the forest, saying, "If you go the way I am advising, it should not be more than 8 kilometers." It was a difficult walk. The rain made matters worse. The earth was freshly plowed and stuck to our shoes. We walked slowly.

It was now 11 PM. We could not see anything. When we came close to houses, dogs barked. We discussed the possibility that we might be lost. We had no alternative but to knock on a peasant's door and ask for directions to Linave, so we would know how to get to Saduw without revealing our destination. Our group got a little too close to a house and we were ferociously attacked by dogs. We knocked on the window, but no one answered. After a louder rap, a woman asked, "Who is knocking?" We asked in Polish, "Which is the way to Linave?" She stuck her head out of the window. Panicking, she answered, "Straight along the road from here, you will come to Saduw and Linave." She added, "I am very scared. We cannot sleep. The *Zhydy* pass by every night and the militia keeps knocking as well. We were afraid that it might be the *Zhydy* again and that they would kill us."

We returned to the rest of the group and all of us

walked straight forward in the direction she pointed. We feared getting lost in the fields, so we continued on the road. Divided into pairs, we moved slowly, some distance apart from each other, looking into the dark night around us. We agreed that, if we met anyone, we would use a quiet cough as a signal; if we were close to houses or orchards, we would spread out between them. When we reached a crossroads, it was very difficult to ascertain our bearings in the dark.

It was 2 PM already and we were desperate. We could see everything around us, but alas, no forest. We decided to inquire again. We approached a small house out on a field. Quietly, we tapped on the window. A gravely voice answered. We asked, in Polish, for the road to Saduw. He answered, "I'll be right out." We immediately called over to Bairel and Chaim who were with the group. They were spread out under the trees, armed with large clubs, prepared for anything that might occur.

A well dressed peasant came out. As we approached he asked, "Who are you?" We answered, "What does it matter? Please show us the shortest way to Saduw." He observed us in the darkness of the night, "I know that you are Jews." We demanded gruffly, "Tell us how to get to Saduw and nothing else." In Polish he shouted to his wife, "Hand out half a loaf of bread." We became suspicious. We whistled, and Bairel and Chaim rushed over. Observing the newcomers, he shouted, "Bairel, you are here, too? Don't you remember me? Yuzek! You have been here more than once." Bairel embraced him, "Yuzek, we came to you!? Yes, God has not abandoned us."

After calming down, we began to understand each

other. He told us that on the same day, he was in Lukacze and Jews were still being rousted from their hiding places and killed. The militia was stealing and fighting among themselves. When a peasant broke into the ghetto and started to loot the houses, a German shot him.

Yuzek's wife came out with a bread and gave it to us. Bairel asked for more and she brought another half loaf, saying that she had no more. We took tobacco from the string on which it was spread outside. We also picked up a few bottles of water. He led us to the road. Pointing to a large dark shadow, he said, "You see that area? That is the forest. It is another three kilometers."

We started in the direction of the woods, getting closer to the black silhouette. The light started to come up. Completely exhausted, we entered a new forest. We continued on in there, until we came to a denser part. We sat down and talked. In a very short time some began to snore rather quietly. Four of us divided the watch by the hour.

FIVE
LIFE IN THE FORESTS AND LIBERATION

We woke up from our deep sleep. Shmuel Kolier was sitting very pensively, looking at his sleeping children. Soon everyone was awake. We sat up. Bairel distributed small pieces to everyone; that was our breakfast. We were more thirsty than hungry. Each of us took a sip of water.

It was noon already. We discussed our search for Jews in the forest. Shmuel, Bairel and I pressed on deeper through the trees looking and listening for every sound, but we saw nothing. It was getting dark. We went back to our people. When we returned, they were growing impatient. We decided to continue together to the edge of the forest so that at night we would be able to get some food.

At the edge, we entered a large hole overgrown with vegetation. It was dark outside and a cool wind was blowing. At 9 PM all four men left the forest. Across the field, not far away we neared a few small houses. Bairel knocked on a window. A peasant responded, "Just a minute." Bairel asked if he had any bread. A woman's voice answered, "I don't have any, go to my next-door neighbor. He baked today." We did as she

Life in the Forests and Liberation   149

suggested, knocked and asked for bread. No one answered. Suddenly, someone looked outside the window and a shot rant out. We could hear the bullet whistle as it passed right by us. We dashed away, dropped and crawled on our stomachs. I could feel cabbages under me, so I took one.

When we returned, we wandered around near the forest for a few minutes and then entered our refuge. The rest of our group cried when they saw us, "Everyone is alive? We heard the shooting." We all sat. It was quiet. Chaim disturbed the calm by peeling the leaves off the cabbage. We had a feast, and we fell asleep, sitting.

As soon as dawn broke, our thirst became unbearable. Sitting in one place availed us nothing. We foraged deeper in the forest. Shmuel's children licked the leaves of the trees. We followed suit, lapping the early morning dew. Walking, we came across wild berries; it was very tasty for breakfast. We went on, not knowing our destination. We looked around all of the time, and pressed on through the forest. The area was lush with large trees. We sat down in a small hole. Everyone of us was deep in thought.

The sudden cry of a child woke us. It seemed that this section was populated, so we had to be careful. The crying was silenced by a low, *"Sha, Sha"*. The word *Sha* seemed curious, because it was cooed with a Yiddish accent. It was quiet once more, and we were very apprehensive. The three of us made our way through the branches and between the trees in the direction of the sound. Suddenly, Shmuel cried, "Here are the people." We noticed people in peasant clothes and covered with blankets. One person was definitely a

Jew. We walked over, and recognized him as Yankel Meizlish. Not wishing to scare them, we spoke Yiddish among ourselves. Our voices were heard and immediately they saw us. Yankel ran towards us and we hugged. "How many are you?" Shmuel told him that Bairel went to call the people together. We all sat down and asked for water. They gave us two bottles.

Yankel told us that so far he, his wife, and three children were saved. He was curious to hear how we got out, and he continued, "When they came to get us, we were not expecting them. We were scattered among the burned homes in the town of Poryck. But when we saw them approaching us, we realized what it was all about. My wife, my children and I went into the barn. My father-in-law placed bundles of grain around us. When the militia stormed into the barn, my father-in-law walked over to them. They immediately asked, 'Where is your family? Where are Yankel and your son-in-law?' 'They are working in the field.' 'Good, soon you will take us to them. In the meantime you will dance for us.' My father-in-law said that he did not know how to dance. They replied, 'You will soon know.' A loud crack was heard and he started to scream. They beat him viciously to make him dance. Then they took him away. We laid this way until late at night when we finally emerged. We set off in the direction Of Ozdziutycze, from there to Koniuchy, then to Svyniukhy. In Svyniukhy, near the home of Efraim Klainer, we were caught by a militiaman. My wife and I pleaded with him. We gave him our fur, and we went to Kandraszke on the hill, from there to the Korytnytsia forest. This was the direction I was given. When we entered the woods, it was daytime. Later I went to a peasant and asked for help. My appearance scared him. Then I called on an important communist named Oleksander Sydun; he refused to talk with me. At night I travelled to Linave in the forest. In the meantime I spent some time with a few Christians I knew. It was very difficult. I was hoping for God's help. From what the peasants said, the situation was very sad. Every day the number of dead increased. Peasants were searching in the forest and, when they caught a Jew, they would remove his clothes then kill him. Besides our terrible thirst, the Torezyn police were raiding the area." Shmuel asked if we could buy food. Yankel said that at night he would try to talk with the peasants and, if possible, they would help. This is how the day passed.

When it got dark, Yankel visited a peasant. Shortly afterwards, he came back with him. When the peasant saw us, he became frightened. Shmuel and Bairel took him a short distance away, and after a little time they returned. They said that they gave him a shirt and a pair of pants. He promised that they would not regret it. Soon after the peasant returned with two breads, a pot of cooked potatoes and a promise of more food on the following day. He sat with us and asked about the ghetto in general. He told us the same things all over again. "Jews are still rousted from their hiding places and killed. They're searching in the forest as well, so be on your guard."

We had dinner and planned to go into a deeper, denser part of the woods the next morning.

In the morning we ventured further inside. We agreed to visit Yankel that evening. In the semi-darkness of the woods we sat down in a hole. The day was passing. We heard shooting from all directions.

When darkness fell, Shmuel, Bairel and I went to Yankel. After a short time, Oleksander came. He looked around quietly and said, "I have a bread for you and one for Yankel. Today, I was in Lukacze. It is difficult to tell what is happening. They are looking for Jews everywhere. They find children. Everyone is severely tortured to force them to divulge where the rest are hiding. Afterwards they are killed anyhow. Dr. Shapira. We already knew who he was: chief surgeon of the entire area. We were aware of what he was capable of doing. It is difficult to find an expert of his calibre. The Germans did not kill him. But today, the regional commissioner himself called him over. When the militia entered the hospital, he was performing an operation. They asked him to accompany them. He asked to be allowed to wash up. He did so quickly and they took him to the regional commissioner. He was in the field near the mass graves. Dr. Shapira, moving closer to the regional commissioner, saw the open pit. He was asked about his work. Dr. Shapira said, 'Why did you call me? Tell me! I am not prepared to enter into a discussion with you!' The last words from the regional commissioner were, 'Yes, you are an undisputed expert in your field, but you are still a Jew. You have no right to live.' And he shot him on the spot. Many peasants mourned his death. He had saved many lives. There was something else. Yesterday, Ukrainians from the village Rafaluwka caught Chaim Pechornik and his sister. They tied them with thick ropes, put them on a sawbuck and cut them to ribbons, starting with the legs." Oleksander observed that some Ukrainians objected, but it was of no

Life in the Forests and Liberation 153

avail. "Now about you. I will no longer bring you any bread. I am scared. If they find out, they will shoot me." Shmuel stopped him, saying, "We know the situation. We are not children." Then Bairel joined in, "We will still give you something else." He became interested. Shmuel returned with a few children's items. Shmuel continued, "You know, Oleksander, what we need now; what is most important to us is life-saving food." Oleksander's mood changed; it was now pleasant. "I'll bring. I'll give."

We continued talking with him, "Maybe you know where there are other Jews." We mentioned many other relatives from Lukacze, Svyniukhy and the rest of the area. He said that he knew them all, and that they were in the forest. We asked him to arrange a meeting with them at the first opportunity. Then he left.

On the following evening he came again. He told us that on the next day he would be in Lukacze, his wife would be in Torezy and he promised he would bring information about what was happening.

Returning to the other people, we discussed our situation. Sitting like this was not a solution. What we were receiving from Oleksander was really nothing. We had to find ways to obtain food from the peasants' fields at night. During the day we searched the forest for more Jews and tried to form friendships.

As the sun rose, Moshe, Shmuel and I entered the forest. We did not know in which direction to go. We went into the most overgrown places. We heard talking and shouting. Listening carefully we ascertained that the majority of the voices belonged to shepherds.

During our walk, we met Christians with axes attached to their belts. It started to rain, which darkened the sky. We returned to our people.

From a distance Batia Pechornik and Shmuel's children noticed us and approached. They asked, "Did you meet anyone?" Moshe answered, "No one."

A slight noise among the leaves attracted our attention. We look around and noticed someone peering at us. We froze. It was difficult to tell who it was. A child of about 12 appeared. He came closer and stopped. He started to cry, shouting, "Jews!" (in Yiddish). We responded quickly, "Yes, yes. Who are you?" "I am from Horochow; my name is Simcha. I escaped after the slaughter."

We received him warmly among us. He sat down and stared at us. His eyes betokened fear. Chasia Pechornik asked, "Where do you come from? Are you alone?" Tearfully he started to tell us, "I am alone. On Tuesday the murders took place. We were 19 people in hiding. We devised a double roof in the attic. The killers did not find us. This is where we sat until Wednesday night. We were thirsty and hungry. The tin plate roof was very hot. I went out for water. A militiaman noticed where I came from. I went to the river to hide until late that night. Then I returned through back paths to warn the people that they were not safe because I was seen leaving for water. They decided to go into the forest. We went to the river to a spot that was covered with thick vegetation. We decided to wait until the following day. It was already too late to continue. At about 11:00 or 12:00 noon, we suddenly heard steps and the voices of young impu-

Life in the Forests and Liberation 155

dent Ukrainians. 'Here in the river were *Zhydy*. Yesterday we found some here, too.' They approached us and went to report their find to the militia. I waded deep into the water, up to my neck and stood there. Soon we heard German voices and the militia, followed by the sound of shooting. I was hiding in the water, afraid to took. I don't know how long it lasted. It got dark and quiet. I returned to where the people were gathered. I found 4 dead people. I looked for my father. I found him lying in the water with his head propped against a root around which was a lot of grass. I went to him. *'Tate, Tate.'* He opened his eyes and whispered, 'Simcha, you are alive?' 'Yes, *Tate.*' Talk was interspersed with many deep groans, 'I am wounded. I have a bullet in my stomach. These are my last minutes. Listen to me, my son. Put your head on my heart. Don't worry. Now you are alone. Hear my last words. Go into the forest. you must ask God to help you survive all of this. You will not be an orphan. Those who remain alive will reap the benefits. The world will be free. After the terrible destruction Jews from all over the world will gather all the orphaned children and take care of them. They will develop them into important people. They will be the living witnesses of an unbelievable tragedy. Go, my child, go into the world.' These were his last words, finished while crying. *'Tate, Tate'* I called to him but I never heard another word from him."

The child's story disturbed us. The child; so young and yet so advanced, developed such a deep understanding and ability to express himself. We were all in tears.

By evening we were terribly hungry. The three of us went to meet Oleksander. It was late and Oleksander was not there. He finally arrived at 11 PM. He gave us bread and said, "I will not come tomorrow. I am scared." Bairel reassured him once more told him that there was no reason to be frightened. Oleksander said that for the barter, his return was enough. Bairel asked him to come on the following day and we would find a way to negotiate something. Bairel asked for news. Oleksander said that his wife had travelled to Torezyn and Lukacze. There was no major news from Torezyn, where she had stood in line at the corporate store to buy some clothes salvaged from dead Jews. The queue was very long. "Today was a bad day in Lukacze. The Germans and the militia seized people in the street and took them to the mass graves. They were forced to carry earth from everywhere to cover and absorb the blood that was leaking from the grave pits. The fresh blood was more than a meter deep, and flowing very copiously. I was there when the Germans were throwing various chemicals. After a few hours, this activity subsided and then the peasants from out of town were permitted to go home. The Lukacze people stayed and continued to throw more earth."

We returned and told our people about the meeting with Oleksander. We decided not to get together with him any longer, because, "He is a cold-blooded murderer. He was depriving us of everything. He was not ashamed to tell us that he bought clothes that belonged to our executed brothers and that the killers were selling for a pittance." We had to move to a new location to hide from him.

Moshe Kolier suddenly took the children, and started

to cry while talking to himself. "The blood; the precious blood of our brothers and sisters seeps from the graves." He screamed, "Why?" Moshe's words affected us greatly. It was very difficult to fully comprehend the reality of all of this.

We were worrying ourselves sick. Our lives were worse than those of the animals in the forest. The darkness of the night seemed to relax us.

At daybreak we started to move to another place. Hunger tortured us. We went into the forest once more. Batia and Pearl joined us. We met shepherds. Batia approached them and asked for something to eat. They appeared to be scared, but they helped. She took one of them aside and asked, "Where do you live? Far from here? Ask your mother to come here. I should like to talk with her," pointing to the side of the forest. Soon a very old woman appeared. She looked around to make sure that no one else was there. She crossed herself a number of times and asked, "What do you want?" Batia said, "Ho, how poor you are! I will give you my shirt and kerchief if you'll bring bread." The woman asked, "How much do you want?" Batia said, "Three loaves." They agreed on two. She was back shortly with the breads and took Batia's things. We returned to the people.

It started to teem in the forest without any sign of abating. We got soaked and started to shiver from the cold. All three of us went to Yankel to learn about a number of things. His children were lying in the covered hole. His first words were, "I no longer have the strength. I sit all day and recite *Tihilim* (Book of Psalms)." As we talked, Oleksander arrived, remarking, "Today you really got wet." He gave Yankel a bread and some cooked potatoes. Oleksander asked, "Do you have anything else for me?" Shmuel said, "At this point, nothing," and then he asked Oleksander for any news about his brothers, Moshe and Zishe. Oleksander said, "No." He reported once more about the killings and robberies and left.

We stayed to talk with Yankel, remarking that every day produced more victims. Yankel repeated what the peasants told him, about the Ukrainian militia and the Germans encircling and searching parts of the forest. There were shootings and stabbings and the women were turned over to the Ukrainians. We returned to our people with all this tragic information. We lit a small fire to day our clothes and keep warm. This is how we fell asleep.

As soon as morning came, we again moved into the forest. Batia met the shepherd and once more asked for the peasant woman. She received two breads and a few small items.

It was now September 20, 1942.

Shmuel and I met two Jews in the forest. They were naked, with wild, unkempt hair and unruly beards, each carrying a small package under one arm. We asked what happened to them. They told us that they were from Beresteczko. "We were a group of fifty. Not having any weapons, we stayed together. A few days ago we were attacked. Many were shot. Some were wounded and were left unattended. A few women were taken to an unknown destination. We caught one militiaman and killed him. Then they rounded up eighteen men. We decided to divide into small groups. We wandered around in pairs. We realized that if we didn't get anything ourselves, we wouldn't have it. We ate various kinds of grass. Sometimes we picked potatoes. With us were Jews from Wolynia, Lutsk, Ludmir, and even from Piciajuw, which was more than 100 kilometers away. Everywhere there was talk about going to Saduw but with what, we had nothing. Besides, the Ukrainians were heartless murderers! They knew every inch of the forest and were guiding the Germans and committing such outrageous killings. It was much worse than it was for the innocent souls who were buried in mass graves. But we must not lose our courage. We have to maintain our strength and doggedly fight for our lives. If not to save them, at least to wreak vengeance for their loss." They asked about our situation. We told them about the children. Time passed.

We returned to our people and told them about everything that happened. The important question was: what should we do now? It was impossible to fight or to stay alive for any length of time in this forest. We decided to go back to the Aleksandrowka woods to remain in close proximity to Lukacze. There were not that many Jews there, but there were many more gentiles whom we knew and who might give us some food. Also, the Saduwer forest was far better known and was subject to many more searches. We had a problem: how could we return by the shortest route? We could resolve our quandary if we met a Christian we knew and bribed him to lead us via the safest route. Batia promised to talk with the peasant woman; maybe her husband would agree to take us through.

We shared our moments of sorrow and talked about the past and about the difficult life in the ghetto, which now comparatively seemed to us to be a hoped-for dream. In the ghetto we at least had our families, with whom we were able to share our feelings and discuss our problems during the difficult times.

We often sat listening to the stories and discussions of those among us, including the children, despite their young age, and especially Simcha, who held everyone's interest. He spoke to the children about life in the ghetto as if he were a much older worldly man. He described how he looked through a crack to see innocent victims being slaughtered, others beaten, and how, after they were slain, their bodies were thrown into large garbage cans, also his escape from the river with another five Jews. He recalled how peasants on horseback chased and caught them, how they were strangled and how the peasants incredulously asked, "You are still alive?" He related how he hid in a pit under a waterfall and was not seen in the dark of night.

The day was coming to an end as we wandered through the forest, gathering nuts from the trees. We became almost indifferent to the sounds of frequent shooting around us. Batia asked the peasant woman about her husband; she promised to discuss it with him.

It was September twenty second. Since our location was known to the shepherds, we started to look for another place. In the density of the forest we found a deep hole and entered it. Batia awaited for the woman. Shmuel told me urgently, "Come, let's go. We will gain nothing by talking." We left.

We roamed through the forest. We were becoming sick from walking for so many hours, and obtaining nothing. We heard steps and laughter. Women were walking near us accompanied by two militiamen.

"Where do we hide?" We considered the tall grass as a possibility. Running away was not a viable option. We hid in the tall grass. They passed us. It was a very scary moment. Fortunately they kept going. The girls passed with the militia right after they did. We rose and Shmuel jumped, "Oh my children. They are headed in the direction of the hole. Our people are lost. They speak loudly in Yiddish." We started to return on all fours. Suddenly, a shot and another one rang out! We froze on the spot. A short time later we reached the hole. All those inside were sitting, pale and very frightened. We remained for a few minutes. When it quieted down, we told them everything. They said that they were talking loudly when they heard the two shots. Chaim Pechornik suggested that we do not sit in the pit, because in the event of an attack we would be unable to escape. His comments were taken very seriously. We left to look for a different location.

The three of us proceeded very carefully. After covering a short distance Bairel became edgy, "Who is groaning here? Did you hear?" We heard a troubled voice in Yiddish, "Oi, oi" and asking for water. We immediately tried to trace the sounds. Searching through the grass we saw a man's body. We approached him. He opened his eyes, looked at us and begged, "Water, water." Bairel asked him, "When were you shot?" He answered, "Right now, while walking." He was wearing a bloody peasant shirt, and wounded in two places, in his leg which was missing a piece of flesh, and in his stomach. It was hard to tell just where the bullet entered; in his chest or his stomach? Shmuel asked, "Who are you?" Quietly, "from Horochow, from Horochow."

Bairel pulled me, "Somebody is coming." We fled at once. The sounds of peasant voices became more audible.

We penetrated deeper into the dense forest where we found a place off the beaten paths and we moved our people. Chaim and Bairel remained to wait for Batia; she wouldn't know where to look for us. A short time later Batia was back with two people. She told us that the peasant woman brought with her a young peasant, she said he was a reliable fellow; he and a friend would lead us. Batia agreed to pay for this service with a pair of pants and 250 rubles. At midnight we would leave for Aleksandrowka. We started to get ready. However, there was one problem that worried us; Zishel Alter was very sick. But, she said that she would flee with us.

It was evening. Batia along with Bairel decided to wait for the peasants. We lit a fire to warm us. At 11 PM Bairel returned very frightened. He told us that two men arrived with guns and bullets. Bairel wondered aloud who they were. We debated if we should go, they could possibly mislead us. We decided to leave after all. There were fifteen of us and, if necessary, we could handle them.

We turned over our belongings to the women so that our hands would be free to carry sticks, our only weapons. Bairel and Batia escorted the young men. We started on our way, one was stationed in the front and the other in the rear. They led us through various paths in the forest and along open land. We passed fields and avoided houses. Zishel was feeling badly; we helped her, but she slowed our progress. We reached a field, rested and ate something. The peasants brought plums. We picked fruit along the way. Bairel asked them about bread. They said they would get it from peasants. They were observing us carefully every step of the way, talking quietly among themselves. We suspected that they belonged to the "other" people. One went to a house and aggressively knocked on the window. A peasant answered immediately. Our guide yelled, "Hand out two breads immediately." The peasant disappeared to get them. They talked quietly, suggesting that if the peasant came outside, he might recognize them, and thus have to pay with his life. They told us that they were the killers. We knew that we had to flee back into the forest and escape from them. In addition, we observed them all of the time.

Walking at this pace, we watched the sun rise. In the distance we noticed a dark area which, we were told, was the Salver forest. With great difficulty we reached the edge of the woods. It was daylight. We sat down. They asked for their payment, and we gave them what we had agreed upon.

They sat down on a large cut branch and started to talk. I lay down, as close to them as possible, without attracting their attention. I could overhear one of them saying, "I am going to Lukacze immediately. If it is impossible to accomplish anything, then you will remain here. It is light so we will be able to see. As a last resort we will strangle them with padding." Their conversation shook me up. I realized that our lives would soon be over.

I rose, approached them from the other side and said, "We are staying here until the evening. Come when it is dark. We will wait for you." My words pleased them, and they left in two different directions.

As soon as they were gone, I told the group what I had overheard and that every moment we remained there militated against us. "We have to get away immediately." Bairel said, "No, no, we will stay here until night. We cannot go now. The sun is shining. Don't become more orthodox than the Pope. You are listening in on too many conversations. What did you do with your thoughts? Have they been productive?" I said, "Friends, without any further discussion, we must leave. There is no reason to waste more words. There is simply no other way. If you don't go, I will do so alone." Chaim, his wife and two sisters announced, "We too are going." Moshe, after thinking it over, said, "Count me in." Bairel, when he heard that everyone was leaving, said, "If all of you flee, so will we. But how can we find a shortcut?" Shmuel said that he remembered a Pole in this forest who was an acquaintance, and he would find out from him.

We went to the house. Shmuel knocked on the window. The face appearing barked, "Who is this?" Shmuel asked him, "Don't you remember me?" "Oh, yes, Shmuel, what do you want?" Shmuel asked him for the shortest way to the forest." He came out and said, "Listen, my friends. Last evening Yankel Meizlish and his daughter were shot here. You shouldn't be here. You must leave right away. You know that I am not your enemy. If you need bread, I will give it to you," and he did. Bairel took some tobacco. He came out to us, pointed to a small hill and said, "From there, you will see a forest some 4 kilometers away. Continue straight ahead as quickly as you can. You won't have to ask anyone for anything. You will not see any houses. These are lands that belong to the *Pomieseik* (large land owner) and they extend all the way to the forest." We started off in that direction with what little strength we had left.

The sun was shining. From a distance we saw peasants and shepherds herding their flocks. It was very difficult for Zishel. We still had a long distance to cover, and the peasants were watching us. After a herculean effort, we reached the forest and sat down to rest. Then we moved deeper into the woods where we sat down to eat breakfast. We had bread but no water. It was very warm outside. After a few hours, it started to rain. Simcha and Weinstein asked for our bottles so that they could fetch water. They argued, "We are children. We are dressed in peasant clothes. We will get water and return." They made sure they knew the way back and then they left. We broke branches, sat down in a hole and used them to cover our resting place. But it was of little help. We were all wet and freezing.

It was already dark and the children were not back yet. We were very worried about them and thought of what might have happened to them. We speculated and wondered about many things. Bairel informed us that his nephew knew where Stachek lived. Bairel was sure that the children were hiding under the straw at Stachek's. We had to wait until morning and then go to Stachek to search for them. We lit a fire and warmed our clothes. But the children had not returned as yet.

At 4 AM it was dark and overcast. We headed in the direction of Stachek's. It was difficult to get our bearings without any light. We came to the house. The men knocked on the window, Bairel told him who he was and asked, "Did you see two children yesterday?"

Stachek replied, "Why do you ask?" Bairel explained that yesterday they went for water and did not return. He was visibly shaken. "They were yours?" "Yes." "It is too late. During the day, two children came to the village. They entered the backyard of a peasant not far from here and took water from his well. The peasant caught them and took them to Lukacze, where the Germans shot them. The peasant's name is Krawczuk. My friend, now everyone behaves this way. You must be very careful. In this forest there are more Jews. They are killed almost every day. The militia searches around here quite frequently. They know that Jews hide here." Bairel asked him for bread. He answered with a groan, "Every night I give. Where will I get so many loaves?" The peasant's wife handed us a bread from the window and said, "Get away from here as fast as possible, so you will not be seen. The Germans are offering a kilo of sugar and clothes to anyone who tells where to find your people." We took some water and returned to the forest.

Coming back to the group, Bairel cried bitterly and screamed, "Our children, our children." The death of the young ones affected us very grievously. Everyone wept painfully. It was impossible to forget the children; Simcha's young life, his mature understanding of it and our terrible tragedy. In every discussion we could hear his words, "I would like to survive, just to live, and plan later to seek revenge for our fallen brothers and sisters."

Shmuel rose hastily, "Brothers and sisters, we are only thirteen now. We don't know who will be left, but let's hope that some of us will. We have to swear that at the first opportunity that presents itself we will avenge

Life in the Forests and Liberation 167

the loss of our children, destroy Krawczuk's family and burn his house."

We entered the forest, found a place and sat down. The weather was changing. Billowing clouds betokened cold weather. At night it grew worse with the frigid winds and the rains.

On September 29, 1942, we started to walk through the forest. The desire to find Jews was overwhelming. Perhaps we would finally be able to find a solution.

In the evening we left our refuge. We called on peasants whom Bairel and Moshe knew. Bairel would enter a house. We stayed in the orchard picking apples while we waited. After a short time Bairel returned. The peasant followed him, whining, "My dear Jews. I am helping beyond my poor means. Every day I contribute five or six loaves. What can I do? I am virtually alone. The village peasants are hunting for Jews for a pair of pants and a kilo of sugar. If you wish to pick apples in my orchard you may do so without asking." We went back into the forest.

At five o'clock in the morning we noticed two people. We were frightened. We heard a voice, "Jews?" We answered "Yes." We then started to talk. They were from the Lukacze ghetto, also. They were members of the ten families that the Soviets seized at the border. They lived in villages near Lukacze. Together we went to our group. They told us that from the time they left the ghetto, they were hiding in there. They seemed to be more relaxed than we. They said, "When we left the ghetto, we were not sure that we would survive. We still harbor this doubt. Our position is that now we can steal, maim and even kill whoever threatens our lives and that of our dear ones.

This is no time to consider morality. This is what we must do. We band together and if anyone comes looking for us we are not scared. We must be careful in the forest. The day before yesterday in the Wynice woods, twenty one people were shot. Peasants turned them in. A few from Kladniev were also lost. Among us was an old mother who was looking for her son. We later learned that he was one of the 21 who were slain. Not being able to bear her sorrow any longer, she went to the burial ground, cried and bitterly pulled out her hair. The police arrived and shot her on the spot. They also caught two children. This is what happens every day. We are not afraid. We will fight to the end. We have made some plans for the winter. What could one be thinking of, sitting like this in an empty field. Dig underground holes and cover them for security. No one should find them. We are small groups, and we meet in one place, so that one group does not know about the other. When the militia seizes anyone, they beat him or her to death in order to learn where other Jews may be found. Since some people are weak, everything can be lost." We talked about many things, and it continued late into the night when they left.

 Their words were encouraging. Looking back, it was very sad. Our group included people of good character which were usually difficult to find. The majority were weak women and children. We fell asleep.

 When the sun rose, we left the forest to pick potatoes in a field. On the way back we noticed a pear tree; we picked as many as possible. The fruit was delicious. We were very pleased with the good taste and it helped to assuage our hunger as well. This is how our lives continued; sometimes we were successful in getting food; at other times, we were not.

Calling on peasants was worthless. There were no new places to try. Too often we were visiting the same peasants. They refused any further help, explaining that it was impossible for them to keep giving every day. In addition, the stealing impacted badly on the area. The militia seemed to know everything, and made leaving the forest more difficult. In many places the militia lay in wait in the forest.

On the night of October 2, 1942, Stachek told us that along the road that passed through the field, two Jews were shot. He did not know who they were. The Kladniever frequently visited us. We sat for hours talking about the same problem: how to save ourselves.

The days were bad. It was cold and it rained at night. It was difficult to find anything to eat in the fields. Days of searching often yielded negative results. The Kladniever in their small groups decided that they would return to their birth places to ease their struggle for survival. There they had Poles and other acquaintances who might ameliorate the situation. After many discussions we arrived at the same conclusion: Without weapons and at the mercy of the peasants for hand outs, we had to look for a more comfortable place for ourselves.

Days passed. The hunger was unbearable. We were living only on watermelons, and even they were not easy to get. Many of us developed chronic stomachaches. There seemed to be no solution to our situation. We sat down to decide on our strategy. Batia and Pearl cried bitterly. "Why are we so unlucky?" I spoke my mind and recommended that we head in the direction of Svyniukhy and Korytnytsia. Shmuel and Bairel had many acquaintances there and I could guarantee bread for three or four people. Chaim and Chasia argued, what if I were killed; since they knew no one they might as well be dead. Under these circumstances, they decided to go in the direction of Lukacze, where they might be fortunate in obtaining something from the peasants. Bairel and Shmuel said that in and around the area of Lukacze they had many more acquaintances than they did in Svyniukhy and Korytnytsia. During the entire discussion, Batia tried to convince Shmuel and Bairel not to leave. I told them that there was no other option and that our destruction was imminent.

On October 5, I lazed around all day. I Lost interest in everything, including the group which was involved in discussions all the time. Life brought us together more inseparably than brothers and sisters. But this was it. The destiny that bound us together, now separated us. We had a pleasant wish, how wonderful it would be, if we could all survive and reminisce about our experiences when we were all safe and free.

Shmuel looked at his watch. It was 8 PM. I stood up and started to say our good-byes. It was difficult to find the right words. Shmuel and his small child, Mechele, came to accompany me. We left the forest and entered an open field. Shmuel said, "I think Korytnytsia is in this direction." We said good-bye. The child hugged me, "Mechel, Mechel, where are you going? Don't leave us. Don't leave us." He kissed me. I embraced and caressed him saying softly, "Mechele, don't cry, we will meet again and everything will be good." I also wept. We separated sorrowfully.

I ran into the fields, avoiding houses and wagons, and when I saw someone, I would lie down. It was raining, leaving our roads very slippery. I removed my boots and slung them across my shoulders, and continued on. A long time passed. I approached a forest, and felt lost. I was scared to enter. I knew that going inside could be my worst enemy in the darkness of the night. It might look inviting to enter, but difficult to get out. I walked straight along the road. I thought that in the absence of light no one would come by. But I did not know where the road was leading me. I noticed a house, and I approached it. In the yard I saw many farm machines. I deduced that this must be the yard of a *Promieseik*. I was scared and left immediately, continuing on my way. After covering some distance I realized that it was useless. I didn't know where I was. I saw a small house, went to the window and knocked; no answer, so I continued on.

Walking this way, I realized that the night was ending. Where would I hide? I spotted another little house. Again I knocked on the window. A voice said, "Who is there?" I asked for the name of the place and where it was. He inquired, "Who are you?" I answered, "It does not matter. Please tell me where I am." The voice, "Again a *Zydzy*, every night, they don't let us sleep." The peasant told me, "This is Cholopicz, on the direct road to Lukacze. It is only 6 kilometers from here. Go away quickly, the militia has been searching around here all night." Frightened, I went on my way not knowing what to do. I was hopelessly lost. To reach Korytnytsia was out of the question. To be alone in the forest, in this unfamiliar and dangerous area, was very frightening.

I thought of going to the ghetto in Lukacze, to find a cellar and lie there during the day. There was no other way. I walked quickly but it was not easy. Severe hunger and thirst made the trip more difficult, but I continued. I saw houses, a sign that I was getting close. But I did not know which section of Lukacze I was in. Many houses already had their lights on. I was scared. The daylight would soon be here. I noticed a large house with many illuminated rooms. I stopped to get my bearings. Everything was unfamiliar. I might possibly be near the town hospital in Lukacze.

It was first light of day when I climbed a small hill and suddenly saw, in front of me, all of the town of Lukacze. I froze. Looking around, I learned that I was a few steps from the police station. I could be caught at any moment. From where I stood I saw a straight road leading onto a hill, on which were houses and an orchard. I threw my boots on the hill, very quickly negotiated the steep walls and walked very fast. I fell into a pit of barbed wife. I felt my pants and my legs tearing. I climbed out and fell into another hole, clambered out, and ran between the trees. I could not stand long. Through a narrow path, I reached the main road near Shainer's house across from the ghetto. Not seeing anyone, I slipped into the ghetto; entering the house of Pesach Schneider, I noticed that everything on the floor had been broken and stepped upon. I felt a terrible pain in the pit of my stomach. I could not stay in the ghetto.

I went back into the street and looked around. I decided to go into the river. I went to the edge and

Life in the Forests and Liberation 173

then proceeded deeper and deeper. It was difficult to find a place in which to hide because all the normal vegetation in the water was crushed and destroyed from being trampled upon. I stepped on and over human bodies in the water. Walking on I came to a waterfall. But what to do? Should I cross, or stay? The other side seemed to have less vegetation. I decided to remain where I was. I leaned my head against some sticks and I lay like that in the water. I heard the sound of chewing, probably a beet. I was not afraid. Perhaps it was a Jew, not far from me.

It was bright daylight, and it got warmer. Hunger ravaged me ceaselessly. I felt very weak. My wounded legs pained me a great deal. I touched my wounds in the dirty water. Time passed slowly. The day seemed interminable.

From a distance, I heard shepherds talking. The sun was beginning to set. The ache in my heart seemed to abate. It might still be possible to get to Korytnytsia. A scream from a shepherd scared me. He called to the others, "Come, Jews, Jews, Every day, there are *Zhydy* in the water here. Today we did not look." I waded deeper into the water with my body totally immersed, but what about my head? I selected a root from under my head and put it over my face. Soon after I heard the shouting, "Here, here." I could not tell if they were near me. I did not hear any steps. I removed the root from my face. Not far away from me, I saw the shepherds lifting a child of about twelve years old, wearing a winter jacket, with the water dripping from him. The *Skucym* (gentile young men) all together carried him.

It was night, but it was early. I removed all my

clothes, wrung the water out of them and put them back on. I stood looking in the direction of the ghetto. It was covered by a hazy darkness, only the houses could be seen. Suddenly, whatever courage I may have had left abandoned me. Without realizing it, I was fearful of everything around me.

I rose and walked towards Shainer's burned out mill. Along a narrow path I crossed the river to the open field away from the road. I proceeded slowly in the direction of Svyniukhy. I was much more relaxed now because I knew the way. I walked at a slow pace, and after some time, I rested for a while. The hunger confused me. All I could think about was reaching Svyniukhy and soon having food. But with my wounded legs it was very hard going. As I trudged along I realized that it was already late at night. My calculations indicated that I had still 6 kilometers to go. With a great deal of difficulty, I reached the first houses of Svyniukhy.

I went to Michael Humans; maybe I would be able to stay there for a day or two to rest and decide my future course. I climbed the hill to a small house. A dog viciously attacked me. I knocked on the window. A woman asked, "Who is there?" I said, "Where is Michalko?" She answered, "He is in the mill." "Tell him that this is Mechel. I am very tired and I want to come in." The woman shook with fright, started to cross herself and said, "Oh God, they will kill us all." I told her not to worry, everything would be all right. The dog did not stop barking and jumping, when suddenly the path to the house was illuminated by flashlights which were coming closer. People were carrying guns. I realized that the situation was catastrophic. I turned into the field and started to run.

I raced away while the flashlights were focused on me. Whenever the rays followed me, I dropped to the ground. When they ceased, I started running again. I was looking for dark spots only where I could hide. I passed a yard and once again a dog attacked me. I hit him with my stick. He screamed terribly and I kept running.

The frantic chase during the night did not stop. They kept finding me with their lights. They shot at me whenever they saw me. It energized me. I kept running on and on but I did not know my destination. One thing was clear: their lights seemed to be getting farther away from me. I accidentally fell into a hole and I lay there. It was quiet. The lights had disappeared. I heard two shots in the distance. I lay like that for a short time. Then I rose to see where I was. In the darkness of the night I groped and touched the vandalized tombstones. My instinct told me that I was among Jews, dead, albeit Jews. (My mother was also buried there.)

Slowly, I descended the hill. I knew this area. I was thinking, "Where can I find a place to hide for two days for some rest?" I decided to set out for Czajko. After walking a few hundred meters, I saw two large lights shining from the mill near my home. The illumination made it easier to find the right direction. I continued through the fields towards the river, crossed it over a small bridge and then slowed down because I was already in town. I heard the grinding sounds of peasants' wagons around the mill.

Using back paths, I arrived at Czajko's window. I knocked. It was quiet. Soon a voice asked, "Who is there?" I said, "Open the window." Antonina Czajko recognized me immediately. She shouted, "Mechel, you're alive, thank God. You will survive." I asked her to open the door and let me in. She hesitated. Czajko rose from his bed, also. Both looked at me and Czajko said, "We are afraid to let you into our house. We have another person, a teacher, living with us and she can hear what we say. If they find out, they could kill us. Go to Korytnytsia, to my brother-in-law, you will be able to stay there. I think that Yecheskel is there, too, and so are other Svyniukhy Jews. I will send you whatever you need." I explained, "I am terribly tired. My legs are lacerated. I cannot go on. If not remain in the house then anywhere else, so I can rest until tomorrow night. I don't want to stay here anyway." They told me that it would be impossible for me to stay there. They were scared. I went across the way to my house, and tried to open the back door. I knew that door for such a long time. It was impossible to open. I went to the window, knocked, called "Strap", but no one answered. I could hear whispering in the room. I talked through the window, explaining, "Only until tomorrow night. Then I will leave. I would like to hide in a part of the cellar that even you don't know about." But no one answered. I returned to Czajko's window. His wife and he were both looking at me. He urged me, "Go to Korytnytsia." I said, "It is already becoming light outside. It is impossible for me to go now." "So go to the river bank which is heavily overgrown with vegetation and sit there until tomorrow evening." I realized that further pleading was in vain. I asked him for some food. He gave me two breads and I left.

Thinking over this meeting, I was bothered. How could people like Czajko behave in such a callous way?

It was daylight. I tried my utmost to get to the Korytnytsia forest. It was too bright to approach peasants at this time. During the day with great apprehension, I came to the forest. I was suffering from unbearable thirst.

I noticed a house near the forest, but I was afraid to enter it. I did not know who lived there. Suddenly, a peasant woman emerged with two pails on her way to the well for water. I asked her for some. She peered intently at me and shouted, "Oh, Mechel, it is you!" I looked at her and asked, "Who are you?" She replied, "What, don't you know me? I am Yakov Babelas's wife." I said, "Oh, yes, I know you." She put the pails down and entered the house. Her husband rushed out. He shook my hand, "Mechel, you're alive!" He looked around and said, "Quick, come into the house."

After entering, he locked the doors. We sat down. The old woman handed me milk and white bread and said, "Eat, eat, don't be shy." I ate heartily; it was quite tasty. Yakov said, "Come into the barn. You are tired. Get some rest." I lay down on the straw. I showed him my torn legs. He brought linen and iodine and bandaged them. Then he asked me to tell him about my recent experiences. I obliged, and without any embellishment related everything I saw. I asked him about other Jews. He told me that the peasants were saying that Yecheskel Greenspan, Yitzhak Pechornik, the two Lichter brothers and Motel Wallach were in Korytnytsia. He added that Shiya Groiss had been in the forest; he entered the house of Iwan Zawodnik to ask for bread while a militiaman was there. The militiaman told him to get out to be shot. Outside Shiya Groiss asked for a cigarette before his execution. His wish was granted, then he was shot. The three Schneider sisters were seized by the militia and were taken to Horochow. Theirs was a terrible fate. At the beginning of the trip to Horochow, they tore off their clothes and pulled out their hair. Nachum Meizlish, Yankel Lichter and a Lukacze boy, Ashkanazi, were rounded up by the militia in the village of Kityw and taken to the Lukacze ghetto. Meir Misuris was in Korytnytsia, too. In the forest were many Jews from the surrounding towns and shtetls. He added that for the local Jews, life would be easier than for the others. He left and I fell asleep.

She woke me and brought food out to me. In the evening he came and said, "I am afraid to harbor you here. When you come to me, I will give you whatever you need, but you have to leave early in the morning." He told me to go to the forest.

At dawn I went into the fields. I was wondering where to go and decided to call on Chwadosc (the brother of Antonina). I came to the window of a small house and knocked. Chwadosc emerged, recognized me and asked, "What do you want?" I told him that I had spoken with his sister. He listened carefully and said, "It is possible that you may be able to stay here, but I would first like to discuss it with my wife and child. In the meantime, go into the forest. Come at night and I will give you my answer." I took a bottle of water and went into the forest.

Life in the Forests and Liberation

It was early in the morning and I was already up and about in the forest. Maybe I would meet Jews. I spent the day searching. I met no one. It was teeming. As soon as it grew dark, I left the forest and returned to Chwadosc. I met him at the gate of his yard. He noticed how wet I was, and said, "I discussed it with my family. Anyhow, stay in the barn. It is impossible to stay here. The barn is open, without a roof. Settle down in the straw. If they find you, I don't know you." I entered the barn and took some straw. He brought me some cooked potatoes, which I finished and fell asleep. At first light he came with his son, asked me many things and told me what I had already heard from Yankel. Exactly where the Jewish people were, he did not know. He informed me that he would soon be going to Svyniukhy to visit Czajko and when he returned, he would tell me what happened.

On the evening of October 8, 1942, he came and told me that two brothers, Yankel and Henick Fichman, were brought into the village. The militia ordered them to dig a hole near the old cemetery. When they refused, they were severely beaten, shot and their bodies were rolled down the hill. Two peasants volunteered to bury them.

Life was difficult. The cold hurt. It was unbearable without food. He threw a few cold potatoes and a piece of bread to me and ran out. He appeared with the look of a peasant to tell about the killings and beatings that were taking place. For days I lay hidden under the straw, so I would not be seen.

On October 13, he came to tell me that on that same day he saw emaciated, hungry and sick parents and small children in the field. They came out of the forest and asked for bread. They were from Horochow.

On October 16, he and his son came out to meet me. They looked at me and said, "You are lying in straw, why do you need your suit? Let's trade, I will give you my linen suit in exchange." I did not know how to respond. I removed my clothes, he took them and in return, gave me his old jacket and pants.

On October 24, at night, I was awakened from a dream-filled sleep. I opened my eyes. Chwadosc and his son were standing next to me. He said, "I want to tell you something. Listen, Mechel, we are scared. We want you to leave. We are really frightened. You know what is happening." I answered, "There is no reason to be fearful. The barn is a long distance from the house. If I get caught, I will not betray you." All pleas were of no avail. "Leave tonight" were his final words. I lay there for some time, unable to fall asleep, thinking, where do I go now?

I went out near the forest. I stood there for some time, not knowing what to do. Remaining in the forest would be a mistake. Without realizing it, I started back in the direction of the village. The fuzzy images in the dark night played a game in my head. It was almost impossible to determine who lived there. I moved closer, believing that this was where Avross Barentchok lived. When I entered the yard, a dog attacked me. I knocked on the door. After a short time, a man came out and asked, "Who is there?" I recognized his voice and I whispered, "Hershel's son, Mechel." He shouted, "You are alive!" "Don't you see?" "What do you want?" "I would like to hide here." My situation was apparent. He paused for a moment and said, "Wait, I am coming out." He appeared immediately, carrying a peasant's cover. He led me into the barn and said, "Lay here until morning. Then we will decide. The dog is a trouble-maker."

The militia was roaming around. The only others who ventured outside at night were Jews. I lay in the barn thinking, will this ever end?

At break of dawn the barn door was opened quietly. "Mechel?" I rose quickly. Avross stood there eyeing me and thinking. He looked sad and started to cry bitterly; it was self-revealing. My plight was becoming more obvious to him. What an unfortunate situation I was in!

He started to talk. "Why do they kill you? I have travelled to many countries. People are everywhere and each one has a right to live. God created the world for all to enjoy." He wiped the tears from his eyes and tried to appear happy, "Don't worry. You will survive. Things won't always be as bad as they are now." He asked me what news I had heard about Jews, and who was still alive? He told me that he was going to church and that his daughter-in-law would give me food. Not too long afterwards she arrived, a big, healthy-looking peasant woman, with a bowl of meat and *kreplach* (dumplings). I ate while she talked a great deal about the Jews who were killed. Where they met their ends and who was still alive. She asked me if I had escaped with my father and my sister Chaike (assuming that they were alive). Her words affected me deeply. My father and Chaike? (I knew that my father would not think of leaving the ghetto. My little sister Chaike was only 13. She refused to go with me under any circumstances.) She argued, "If we stay together, neither one of us will survive." She was kissing me incessantly and, with tears in her eyes, sobbed, "Mechel, go alone, it is the only chance you have for surviving. I am going to the mass graves, confident that you will live to tell the world about the tragic things that happened." These were her last words to me.)

Impatiently, I awaited the return of Avross. Before noon he returned in a good mood. He talked with me in a very friendly manner. "How are you doing? Did you eat? I will help you in whatever way I can. Let's hope that you will survive. From what we hear from the peasants, your father and sister are alive." I asked him how he knew this. He answered this was what people believed. He left.

After some time he returned with food. The morning meal made me sick. He kept repeating, "I will help you. You have to remember that I have a family to think about and we are scared. Now, down to business. Outside, next to the barn wall are two stacks of straw. It is impossible for anyone else to get near them. You will go to the barn wall into the straw and settle down there. We will open a board in the barn wall through which we will give you food."

As soon as it grew dark, Avross and his son, Michalke, entered the barn. Making preparations, they gave me an additional cover. The son checked to see if anyone was near. He ran in, "Come quickly, we don't see anyone now." I went out, climbed a tall ladder and jumped into the center of the straw. I let go and dropped down. Avross did the same. Together we pulled the straw so we could get to the back. Avross said, "From now on you are called Michalke, like my son, so that no one will guess that we have a stranger here." He pointed to the wall of the barn, "From here you will receive food. Lay quietly. Whatever I hear, I will tell you. If I meet any Jews, I will call you together."

Lying under the straw was not bad. There was enough food. The difficulty was loneliness. A day seemed like a year. We suffered through sleepless nights. Every day when Avross brought my food, I asked for news. He gave me news about the shootings only.

On October 27 at noon Avross brought food and told me that he would soon come out to me. I thought that it was probably not easy for him and that he would ask me to leave. I waited impatiently. After a short time, he arrived. He put his head through the opening and whispered, "I will tell you something. There was a massive raid by the Germans and the militia in the Saduw forest. Many Jews were killed. A great number of bodies are lying around. They brought 6 Jews: Hershel Linver, Alter Ingber, Laib Zemel, and three others I don't know to Svyniukhy. They were jailed for the night. Today a member of the gestapo came from Horochow and killed them near the old cemetery. Many fled into the forest. Others ran away, wounded. Among them was Gittel, Hershel Linaver's daughter; she had a bullet in her arm. In addition, there was Shive Wallach, but I don't know too much about her. That is all. I will report to you when I learn more." The information shook me up. The killings were impossible to comprehend.

Life under the straw was quite confining. My thoughts tortured me. When would it all end? Despite the difficulties, I did not look for another place to hide. It was cool outside and raining everyday. I dug a deeper hole in the straw to prevent getting soaked from the rain. Every time Avross arrived, he brought news but it was always the same. Every day in the forest he saw wounded and hungry Jews all pleading for bread. This kind of information belied the belief that a change was a possibility.

On November 13 Avross came and asked me about my plans. The weather was getting colder and the winds were becoming more damaging. Maybe I should go somewhere else. I asked him to let me stay, in spite of everything. After a short pause, he looked at me and said, "I would like to save you. I will try something else. We will fill the barn with straw, and at the wall we will prepare a small corner for you. To be able to get to the wall from the outside, we will cut a small opening through the straw. A board will be removed from the inside, through which you will get food. It will probably be dark for you in there." He left and I heard them working in the barn.

On November 21 at dusk Avross arrived. In the straw we removed the board from the barn, and I moved into the corner. He gave me a hammer, nails and a board to close the opening. I would have to take the food from under the second board, then close it also. I entered and I made a refuge for myself.

In this grave-like space, it was always fearfully dark. I knew every hour of the day or night. The poultry were my best clocks. Much more unbearable were the dirt and lice which were attacking and eating me ravenously. It was impossible to fall asleep. They infested all the rags, and the mice too became my unwelcome tenants. They were climbing all over me, feasting on even the smallest piece of bread that happened to be near me.

On December 14 Avross visited again, and asked me to leave. He said he had only one son and a grandson and he did not wand to jeopardize their lives because of me. He talked about the times, and said that for the slightest infraction, people were receiving death sentences. I answered, "Naturally, I would like to survive but even more than that, every Jew who escapes death is interested in the life of his savior more than in his own. Let's hope that times will change and that the truth will triumph. Let's continue the struggle and not lose our courage. We are the ones who suffer, and you know our condition, but we still hope for the day when the torch of freedom will shine again. Our fight for life is more bitter than can be imagined. We live under terrible conditions, hungry, dirty, and loathed. We suffer more than animals in the forest. Every affronted humane person has an obligation to attest to the barbarism of the heartless monsters. Whenever life is at risk, can any commensurate payment be made for its suffering? Also can those who actively strive to save a victim, really thoroughly understand the situation?" My words affected him. He was thinking and left with a moan. I suffered from lack of sleep.

On December 26 the weather suddenly turned very cold. I wrapped myself in rags but it was still unbearable. Avross called frequently and asked me how I was bearing up in the frigid climate. I told him not to worry about it. "Just let me stay here." My shirt and pants were threadbare and rotten. With every movement of my body, I was exposed. But as far as I was concerned, I was happy. My struggle steeled me to remain adamant in my resolve to continue my fight against the bastards. I told myself, "Get revenge!" This was a major reason for the struggle. But the lice, the blood suckers; every day they tortured us.

On December 31 Avross brought me a cover; he said that he had made it during the day for the New Year. He left and immediately returned with food and a few utensils. He handed me a glass. I smelled liquor. I gave it back to him. He urged, "Drink for me." I did. He started to cry and sobbed, "Oh, why do you suffer so much? Can no one understand your plight? No, no." Suddenly, his expression changed, "Don't worry, Mechel. Let's drink to the annihilation of Hitler and his murderous gang. Although your father and sister will not be alive on that day, the victory will come." He left.

The New Year imbued me with a great deal of courage in imagining a better tomorrow. But soon the worrisome though about a new hiding place, returned.

In recent days the conversations with Avross were very brief. Whenever I asked for news from the forest, he would just say, "Bad." When he did speak less curtly, he said, "Generally, it is the same thing. Sick and freezing women locked in each other's arms could be seen under bundles of straw."

January 15, 1943, was a frigid day. I asked Avross about how to combat the mice. After thinking about it for a moment, he said, "I will not supply you with poison. But I will bring you two cats, maybe they will help." In the evening he brought them. I sat covered in my rags. With my every turn, a cat jumped or a mouse was squashed. It was wild, and it continued this way late into the night. In the morning I threw out the cats and searched around me. Whenever I found a mouse, I would toss it right out. When Avross brought me food and saw the rodents outside, he asked, "Where did so many come from?"

On January 24, the cold was becoming more severe. I was freezing. I felt it mostly in my legs. I became drowsy but I fought sleep. The cold frightened me. I vigorously rubbed my legs to keep them from becoming frost bitten.

I felt a terrible frigid wind whistling around me. It was torturous waiting for the day time. Suddenly, a light appeared in my confining "grave". I did not know its origin. I looked through the cracks, the wind had blown the straw off my "nest". Suddenly I heard three knocks on the board. I opened it quickly, Avross shouted, "Are you alive?" and then he crossed himself. "It was scary outside. Did you see what happened during the night? The whole roof blew off and the straw with it. Is any part of your body frozen?" It seemed that my legs were numb. "What can we give you to help?" He left and very quickly returned with a bottle of alcohol and a pot of hot coffee. I ate and drank and then I wanted to sleep. I covered myself well and dozed off.

Avross's voice woke me. He told me that he and his son worked all day to put the hiding place back together again. He brought me alcohol, and told me that it was calm outside and that he hoped that the coming night would be less harrowing for me. It was not as cold. Avross worried a great deal at that time. He said that he did all that he could possibly do so that I would be all right. He told me that now wherever they go, all they hear is talk about how Jews froze under straw.

The peasants were talking about all the surrounding areas. From Svyniukhy, Gittel Linver and Avraham Schwartz were recognized, though frozen to death. The hope was that such cold weather wouldn't return.

On February 1, Avross came running in scared. Germans and the militia arrived to seize people for forced labor in Germany. He said, "Nail the board and cover it with straw. You know our signal. They might come into the yard searching, so be careful. We are escaping into the forest." I tightened and secured everything. I sat quietly, listening for the slightest noise. Whenever the dog started to bark, I was almost certain that someone was in the yard. This is how the day passed. In the evening, Avross came to me, and told me that they did not come to this area. The Germans went to the region of Stelmach and seized a few victims there. The rest had fled. He said that what the Jews said before they were slaughtered was true: "From us they made the flour and with you they will knead and bake."

We were blamed for every event that occurred.

Every time Avross called, he asked one question: "When are you going to leave?" The situation was becoming critical with the frequent arrivals of the Germans in the villages. The peasants became panicky, with the greatest fear prevalent among those who were hiding Jews. The thought that always tortured me and never stopped worrying me was, "Why doesn't it end, this life in a 'coffin' with all the mice, lice, darkness and weaknesses?" Quite often I would lose confidence in the hope for a happier tomorrow.

On March 15, Avross visited in a happy mood. The

militiaman who killed the first Jew to leave the ghetto was shot in the street in Lukacze. "The blood of your brother does not rest." After a short pause, Avross continued, "There is something terrible I have to tell you. It will be better if you hear it from me. Six days after the mass slaughter, Andrii Blecher found the corpses of your brother Meir and his son Yankele (11 years old). He took them to the mass grave site and told your brother to dig a hole. He refused, crying and screaming. Blecher beat him severely and threatened, 'I will kill your son first so you will see it and then I will kill you.' He shot the child first and then your brother. Afterwards Blecher returned to the village and told everyone what he did. Mechel, don't forget it." (This was added later.)

On March 28, Avross came to me, elated, and in great detail, reported that the militia was abolished and that there were many partisans, but he did not know who they were or what their goal was. "The end of the German beasts. The peasants were saying that the German army was defeated at the Volga near Stalingrad. Hundreds upon hundreds died. Hitler said that Russia, the United States and England signed a joint pact against Germany." Now Avross began to rant feverishly. "One more loss and he will flee. Now, Mechel, let's talk about ourselves. You lived through the worst of winters here. It was still quiet. Now there are partisans or new groups, the Germans will show up more frequently. It would be far better for both of us if you are not captured. I did everything I possibly could for you. Now I want you to leave. You may stay here until April 1."

Avross's words brought me some measure of happiness. If the public talks repeatedly, there must be some semblance of truth in their stories. I had the privilege of hearing about the first evidence of Hitler's downfall. But about my own situation, various thoughts occupied my mind. It was difficult to decide where to find a place for myself. If it was true about the partisans, and the moment of their revenge for our blood that was spilled, then we will put everything else aside. But it was not easy to tell.

When Avross came, those same questions were raised. He repeated, "The end of Hitlerism is imminent." He spoke about the partisans with great excitement and pride, about their activities and about how they seized arms from the Germans. He was not sure if Jews were among them. After some effort, I learned from his son, Michalke, their political aims. They wanted to create a free Ukraine. They hoped to realize the goals and ideals of Petlura, Wlasow and Bandero. There were disagreements among them, too. [Historical note regarding pogroms—Chmielnicki first organized pogroms against the Jews. Petlura continued them during WWI. Bandero reintroduced them in 1939 and Wlasow continued them during the second half of WWII.] After I heard all of this, it was evident to me that for Jews, the burdens were far from light. Who knows if the struggle might not be even more burdensome. One thing was clear: in time we would be enlightened.

On March 31 at breakfast, Avross visited with his son. He advised me to leave during that night. I had been ready for this for a long time. I never once forgot that this moment might come. But it was very taxing in any event. Where would I go? At noon Avross brought me a package. "Take this and get dressed. In here are underwear, a shirt and pants." All homemade from patched-up linen. "Put it on." At dusk he came back with his son. "Are you ready?" "Yes." I pulled out the board and slipped out. My subconscious longing was for the "grave". I would have preferred to stay there until the end. He led me through the orchard, we said good-bye and he said feelingly, "Go. Let God help you. Don't go into the forest. Be careful of the new partisans."

It was hard to bestir myself after such a long time of lazing about. The fields were waterlogged. Pieces of mud were sticking to my shoes and I was sweating. But where should I go? I thought about many acquaintances and good friends in the area. I started in the direction of Chwadosc's house. I got close to it, looked through the window, and when I saw no strangers, I went right in. Upon seeing me, Chwadosc jumped and said, "You are alive?" I didn't answer. I asked a few questions and he imparted the same news that I already received from Avross. He told me that Chaim Misuris was alive and that he saw him in Korytnytsia. I asked him to let me stay for a few days. With an angry look he said, "With me, no! You know what is happening now? It is much worse than it was before. The militia fell apart. The Germans are driving through the area daily. Our militia is opposed to hiding Jews." I realized that my requests were falling on dear ears. I continued on.

It was very difficult to decide where to find refuge. I headed in the direction of Anton Trufimyuck's house. I entered and as soon as he saw me, he became nervously fearful. He seemed confused. I talked with him, "I need your help now." His answer was immediate. "I am scared. I have a wife and a child." I pleaded, "Let me stay in your barn under the straw. Whatever happens, I will not betray you." After a lengthy discussion, I entered the barn.

It turned bitterly cold, the streets were covered with deep snow. Once a day he brought food, but very little. He kept repeating, "Go from here. Go from here."

On April 8 I left. When I reached Anton Sztul's house, I went in. Here again, fear was prevalent. I appealed to his conscience, and to his intellect, since he was an intelligent man. I knew that he was a believer, too. He was an active member of his church, and had a better understanding. So he allowed me to stay in his rather small barn. He behaved humanely in every regard. In the morning, after I slept through the night, he came and talked with me. He tried to convert me to his Christian Evangelist sect so that he would be able to intercede in my behalf and enable him to ask his leadership to help me. I argued, "Let's assume that my Jewish beliefs are wrong. So, we will appear before God, you in heaven, and I, in hell, but since you are risking your life for me here today, won't you help me up there, too?" Laughing, he said, "You are too clever." (This was added later.) "The situation is a very dangerous one now. Since there is no militia, the Germans are enforcing order in their stead. They eliminated the previous guards and they are doing away with people about whom they hade the slightest suspicion. Last night in Korytnytsia, they surrounded Arsimstick's house. His entire family was present. They were told to lie on the floor and then they shot them. See how God did not forget the worst murderer of all in this area? The blood of dozens of people were on his hands. Those who helped him were also killed. Now, my dear, I am asking you to leave. You can see that there is no room here." I realized that the time was short. I had to continue on. His information made me happy; the time for revenge had begun.

On the evening of April 13, while looking for a place to rest, I called on Iwan Misjuk. I asked for his help. Looking at him, I realized that I could not stay there. "If my family is at risk, I will kill you right now." I went farther. It was dangerous to move at night. The barking of dogs in the area was a sign that the marauding gangs were active. I heard shots as well.

I went to Yakov Lazar. I repeated my request to him. I knew that it was of no use, and left. Where should I go? It was apparent to me that it was not just where to go, but where to stay for at least that night. Walking in the field near Iwan's house, I noticed the remains of a small razed building. I entered, planning to remain there until the following evening. Everything was broken inside. I sat down in a corner. As soon as daylight arrived, peasants were visible nearby. I covered myself near the wall to avoid being seen.

As soon as the sun went down, I started through the fields in the direction of Korytnytsia. Peasants collecting their tools on their way home, stopped and followed me with their eyes. When I came to Korytnytsia, I waited near the church for darkness to descend. I then went to Makar Ganirovsky and asked him if I could stay there. I reminded him of our old friendship, but he refused to hear about it. Even his wife asked him to help me. I ended up in the potato field. Life there was very bitter and he drove me out.

On April 17 I was forced to once again visit Iwan "the longer" (his nickname). After some earnest pleading, I stayed there. He told me, "Chaim Misuris was there too." He informed me that there were still some Jews in Ludmir and that all the peasants were talking about them. He further added that there had already been massacres in Ludmir, but that a small number of Jews had survived. It was hard to know under what conditions they existed.

I wanted to meet Chaim Misuris to help him in his forlorn situation. Iwan spent many days talking with me. He repeated almost everything I had known for a long time.

On April 24 his wife adamantly insisted that I leave; or, she threatened to turn me over to the gangs. I left.

I continued in the direction of Sydunn's house. As I was passing through the fields nearing Sydunn, I saw him riding toward me on a wagon filled with trash. He recognized me, and feigning talking to the horses, he told me, "Go into the small forest and come over to see me at night. You might meet Chaim Misuris." Peasants who noticed me screamed, "Get out of here, *Zhydy*. Do you want us killed?" I quickly ran into the small forest. I walked very cautiously, looking about at every corner, hoping that I might find somebody; but, nothing.

At dark I tried Sydunn's house. The dogs barked. He came out and motioned me to follow him. We walked in the field to a hole containing winter potatoes. His first words were, "You are alive? The story I heard was that you were shot by the militia in

Humans's fields." I answered in short, "I am alive and I would like you to help me stay that way. I'm sure that I don't have to explain to you what is going on now. I also believe that you are an enemy of the executioners." He looked at me and said, "Me. An enemy? You are wrong. I am not their enemy. And I believe it should remain as it is." His words surprised me. Is this the way a person who was an outspoken communist for years speaks? He gave me a bottle of milk and a piece of bread. I ate it unenthusiastically. He said, "Chaim Misuris came here last night. He stayed in the small forest for a few days. If you wish, you may stay in this hole of potatoes. I will give you a piece of bread." Then he added, "Shlomo, Yankel Lichter, and Motel Wallach are hiding not far from here."

These experiences with the peasants destroyed my regard for human beings. I sat in the hole and tried to comprehend what had happened to the meaning of the word 'human'. Had compassion descended to animalism? Was all the murderer's poison now sugar-coated? I sat in the hole afraid to go out at night. All day I sat covered in a corner among the rotting potatoes to keep from being caught.

Before the sun disappeared, I left and proceeded in the direction of Iwan's. I entered his barn through the broken board and lay down in the straw. When it got dark, I fell asleep. Early in the morning I heard footsteps. I saw Iwan moving about in the barn. I coughed quietly. He looked around. I raised my head, and he recognized me. He asked out I was. I answered, "You can see." He immediately told me, "If my wife sees you, it will be the end. Better leave during the day; at night, if no one sees you entering, you can stay through to morning." I asked him for bread. He got some for me and said, "Flee as fast as you can so people will not notice where you came from." I left and entered a small forest, not too far away. Cattle were feeding and I met shepherds wherever I went. In the evening I repeated the manoeuver and I left early in the morning so that even Iwan wouldn't see me. I went into the fields where there were no houses.

It was very difficult to hide. The hunger and cold were severe. When it got dark, I called on Iwan once more. I was restless during the night. Where should I go? Early in the morning as Iwan came into the barn, I met him. He looked at me and seemed upset. I asked for bread. He said, "I will give you some. But you know I am scared." After he let me have a piece of bread, I returned to the forest where the shepherds noticed me. Every now and then another one was observing me. It was evident that the peasants knew that a Jew was there, and they came to look at me. I realized that the ground was burning under my feet.

A little shepherd came over to me, "Who are you? A Jew?" "Yes." "From where?" I asked, "Who are you?" He answered, "I am Andrii Zilins'kyi's son." "Do you live far from here?" He pointed to a place nearby. I said, "Be a good boy, and bring me a piece of bread." He told me that his grandmother wanted him to take a piece to me, but that he was too fightened to do so. He left and returned with bread. He asked me once again, "Where do you come from?" "I am Hershel's son, Mechel from Svyniukhy. Go and tell your grandmother." Every day thereafter the shepherd brought me bread. I felt that my hours there were numbered. I asked the shepherd, "What are they saying about me at home?" He said that his grandmother wanted to see me. I told him that same evening that I would visit them and they they should not be scared.

On May 3 as soon as it got dark, I went there. As I neared the house, the barking of the dogs brought out a young, strong-looking peasant. He looked me right straight in the eye and said, "You are Mechel?" I observed him closely. He was not one of the friendly peasants. He asked me into the house and offered me food and drink. He sat and told off-color anti-semitic jokes for my benefit. Presumably, for him, I was an exception. I asked him to let me stay in the barn for a few days. "Lay there, who cares. The place is full of holes anyway. If anyone catches you, you are on your own. In addition, the barn is far out in the field. There is no shortage of bread here." The shepherd took me to the barn and said, "Find a place. You will be here a few days." I entered and in the dark I groped through the straw to find my way. I lay down and fell asleep immediately.

I felt someone shaking me to wake me. I opened my eyes to daylight. An elderly peasant woman stood near me, urging, "Mechele, eat something." She sat down near me and began to cry, calling out the names of all the members of my family. "Pity! Why do you suffer so much? I know about the terrible things that have happened to you. Avross, my husband, told me everything. How you almost froze, and about the winter you stayed in a 'grave' with all the animals. That is how you lived." She talked about the unbearable suffering of the Jews in general, and left.

Andrii came in and asked me to fix something for him in the *sieckarnia* (a large instrument used to cut hay for cattle). I worked in the barn repairing it. The work made me feel better. The children, Iwan and Pavluck, were near me every free moment. They asked about everything and they told me a number of things as well.

On May 21, early in the morning, a very frightened Andrii came. He said, "Mechel, you know the partisans? They burned the bridge in Svyniukhy! It is almost a foregone conclusion that the Germans will arrive. I would like you to leave. First go into the grain field, and at night we will decide what to do." I went where he told me and lay down. When it got dark I entered the barn. Soon after, the peasant woman brought me food and said, "Andrii insists that you leave, but wait another day or two." I realized that I had a strong influence over the children and that they could, in turn, win over their father to allow me to stay. The grandmother told me that the children did not want me to leave.

On May 30 Andrii told me that in Sokal and in other villages in Galicia where Jews still lived, the Germans were relishing their latest slaughters. Everything was repeated: the Jews in the forests and the predators killing them everywhere they found them. The tragedy was obvious: the murderers' blood lust was at its peak, although they were clearly defeated.

On June 1 the old grandmother came in tears, "Dear Mechel, I would like to tell you something but don't cry. Your cousin Chaim Misuris was shot today near the Stelmach, close to the forest. The gang appropriated his suit and shoes. The peasants buried him. What will be the end of all of this?" She continued to talk and cry interminably. "Chaim was a good child.

He wandered around with frozen hands and feet and was shot nevertheless."

The gangs virtually owned the villages. It was much more difficult under them than it was with the Germans. They knew every foot of the village and forest. The peasants looked upon the gangs as liberators. It provided a very crucial psychological dilemma. This, of course, made it unbearable for the Jews who roamed about.

On June 10 Avross visited me accompanied by Andrii, who asked me to leave. He was afraid for his family if I was caught near him. Andrii left. I asked Avross to convince Andrii to permit me to stay. I described my situation to him as perhaps only he night understand. He left and then returned in a little while to tell me that for now I was staying. "I will bring you food and as to what will happen later, we will see." He told me that there were still some Jews in the Ludmir ghetto.

On June 11 the grandmother came to let me know that the shepherds met two Jews from Sokal in the grain field that day not far away. She gave me half a bread and told me to see them. I left quickly to look for them in the grain field. The desire to see Jews was virtually impossible to explain in words. I kept looking farther away. Searching in this way, I covered a large area but I found no one. When it got dark, I returned with nothing. I was extremely sorrowful. I wanted to express at least in a word or two, my feelings about our destruction. The thought that my father and my sister, Chaike, might be alive made me restless. Was it true?

On June 20 I decided to go to Czajko. I might learn

something there. After dark, I quickly went to the edge of the river to his house. Along the way, noticing my house and those of my neighbors, made me fearful and nauseous. I saw Czajko near the stable. He noticed me and we entered the house, locking the windows and doors. I immediately asked him about my father, Chaike and other Jews he knew. He repeated what he had heard, that they were alive as was Yitzhak Pechornik, his wife and child. He again told the story about Chaim Misuris and the two children from Kladniev who had lived among the pine trees all this time. The peasants hid them but only last week they were murdered by the gangs. He also told about Zishe Shuster, his brother, Israel, and sister, Devora, Shive Wallach, Shlomo Walter and a few other Jews from Lukacze and Horochow, totalling fourteen, who went to Ludmir in the terrible cold spell and were killed there. In Ludmir, after massacres, some Jews remained alive. He did not know how many. Night fell and I fell asleep.

In the morning the sun shone brightly. Everything was vibrant. Through a small opening of the curtain, I saw our house and the orchard. Everything seemed alive as if nothing happened. Mrs. Czajko brought me food. She was disgusted with everything that was happening.

Later a few peasants entered the other room. A discussion ensued. The entire discussion centered around Jews interspersed with vitriolic and antisemitic expressions like, "There are still too many alive in America and in England." They mentioned who was killed at the mass graves. As soon as they left,

Life in the Forests and Liberation 201

Czajko and his wife came in, embarrassed that I had overheard all this. He stated that those were typical conversations, and mentioned that the murderers poisoned the atmosphere. For evil people the poison needed only a short time to take effect. When it was dark, I went back to Andrii.

One thought that continued to torture me day and night; "Where should I hide?" It bothered me constantly. I saw all of the peasants of the area in my mind's eye. I was trying to imagine if I could have stayed with any one of them. The result was most disturbing.

On July 3 the gangs disseminated flyers warning that anyone hiding Jews would be exterminated along with his entire family. "Every Jew and German is our enemy." The grandmother came crying, "What do you say now? Andrii wants you to leave." I told her that I would like to see Avross and then decide what to do.

On the evening of July 12, the child Iwan told me that two gang members seized his father, the wagon and the horses. They also took axes and pitchforks. He did not know where they went. I could not rest all night. Shooting from nearby continued through the night. After 12 PM the shooting intensified. Impatiently, I waited for the morning.

At daybreak I heard the wagon and horses returning. After a short time, Andrii's wife entered crying. She hugged me and said mournfully, "Mechel, we are all lost. The Germans will kill us all. Last night the gangs attacked the Poles in the villages and killed all of them. They were slain by guns, axes and pitchforks. Andrii overheard the killers last night claiming that they murdered thousands all through the Ukraine. Many escaped into the cities and forests. Now what?"

The news about the Poles dashed my last hope. The Jews trusted them somewhat. They were a minority, like the Jews. In addition, it would cause an upheaval and it would be more dangerous to move around.

The children and the grandmother all arrived and they were scared. At noon Andrii came. He told me, "Be independent." About the events, he said in an amicable way, "Why do you have to suffer? It is impossible for you to survive. I don't know if even one Jew will make it."

A short time later the grandmother entered, crying, "Mechel, about 50 people are on their way. Escape!" I fled to the grain field. After covering some distance, I stopped. I could hear voices coming closer. "Look, look carefully for any rotten Polaks!" I quickly crawled back. I entered the barn through a hole. I saw a long row of them coming towards the barn. Where could I hide in there? The barn was empty and there was no place for refuge. It was hopeless. This was the end! I took out the small bottle of poison that Dr. Torbeezko had given me. I was determined that they would not take me alive. I leaned against the *sieckarnia*, my hand holding the poison near my mouth, talking to myself. "This is the end. What's done is done." They were rapidly approaching the barn. I heard them asking, "Are there any Poles here? They may be hiding but we will find them." I heard the grandmother say, "No, my dear children." The barking of the dogs disturbed my hearing their conversation. They continued to talk. I heard steps moving slowly away from the barn.

After a few minutes, the grandmother entered, kneeled and started crossing herself. She said, "You are not human. You are an angel. Ho, how could they miss seeing you! This place is so hole-ridden! They must have been blind not to find you! But God, God is with you! You will live. Oh, yes you will." Soon afterwards Andrii, accompanied his wife and children arrived. All of them looked at me. Andrii offered me his hand. "Mechel, I am not a believer, and I don't know what to say. Today I predicted that you would not live. But after this, yes, you will survive."

The grandmother went to Avross. He came immediately. Tearfully, he hugged me. "Mechel, I will do anything for you." We continued to talk. He told me that he decided to take me back. But how could I get there? Every place was under the diligent surveilance of the gangs. He had no idea, but decided to come for me with his wagon. I would lie in it, covered with sharp, prickly weeds to dissuade anyone from searching the wagon.

On July 15 Avross arrived. At dusk I was already with him. He hid me in the sheep's long feeding box which was pushed into a corner. I lay at the bottom. Above me was a blanket and on top of that, the sheep's feed. Every day brought news of panic and stories of death. Now, many Polish villagers were the prime targets of recent events. There were reports of Ukrainians seizing Polish girls in the woods, raping them and then pushing empty bottles into their vaginas, and torturing them to death. "First they did this dastardly thing to the Jewish girls, then to the Polish ones," Avross commented. (This was added later.) The difficult tragic events, suspended between life and death, increased my belief in the sanctity of life while enhancing my own desire to live. I thought of the adage that for every plague, there must be a solution.

On August 22 Avross arrived. "Run quickly. The area is teeming with Germans." I got out, but where to go? Armed German vehicles were patrolling the forest. I moved in between the potato plants, not far from the house, and lay down in a hole.

There was turmoil all around me. I heard the screaming and commands of the Germans. They were getting closer to me. I could hear vehicles approaching and others father away. Shortly afterwards, the sounds of light artillery aimed at the forest, started. Every attack was audible to me. The Germans searched in the potato field. I feared that it was only a matter of time before I was caught. It was extremely hot and it seemed to be very early. The pattern of shooting and stopping was repeated all through the day. The Germans were getting closer to me by the minute. My end was imminent and the time passed slowly. My only thoughts were: how do I last into the night? and when will it be possible for me to get out of here? Night arrived.

From time to time rockets illuminated the area. There seemed to be no way out, and the risk of losing my life became a realistic probability. I crawled away from the voices near me. When the sky was illuminated, I lay quietly. This is how I got away from them. Then I continued to inch along on my hands and knees for some 100 meters. I rose and started to walk. I did not know where to go, but obviously it had to be away from the forest. I was in the area of orchard keepers' houses and entered an orchard some distance from a house in which to hide. I ate some fruit, and fell asleep.

Suddenly, I heard the ack-ack of machine guns! The orchard was well lit and the shooting continued. The peasants, in panic, started to run. I got out and ran along with them. It was a dark night. The peasants were talking and cursing the Germans. "What, they want to eliminate us? Like the *Zhydy*! We will not let them. They locked the *Zhydy* in ghettos, but we are free." Out on the road, I finally realized where I was. But again, where to go? I started in the direction of Andrii. Approaching his house, I heard a group of peasants. I went to the well to drink. Andrii came over, "How did you get here?" He looked around and said, "Get under the pile of straw and sit there." Early in the morning the grandmother brought me food. Andrii was scared and urged me to keep going.

On August 25 I went back to Avross. He told me to hide outside in the potato field. Avross's mood had changed. I did not know the reason. I realized that staying with him was impossible. As amicably as he had treated me before, he suddenly became antagonistic.

On September 1 I went to Andrii. Life at his place was precarious, and I had to leave.

On September 6 the Germans re-entered Korytnytsia. Panic was rampant. When the Germans came, it was strangely better for the Jews. Their presence engendered a few days of relief from the gangs. That made it possible to change our location.

On September 22 I called on Lazar. He told me to hide under the straw in the part of the house that was not as yet completed. I buried myself deep in the straw. The shepherds on his land were virtually dancing on top of me all day long. They could have discovered me at any moment.

On October 1 I visited the Kastinowicz house. They allowed me to stay for a few days. The attacks increased. Every day Germans and Russian Cossacks drove into the villages. The peasants panicked.

On October 11 I returned to Lazar, and on the 12th, Lazar came to me with two men, Yura Niticuk and Szurko Trufimyuck. They asked how I was faring. I told them of my situation. When Lazar left, Trufimyuck told me that for two days I should burrow deep in the straw, and that he would come to pick me up, but cautioned me not to tell Lazar.

On October 14 very early in the morning, Trufimyuck and Yura Niticuk appeared. They told me that they would lead the way and that I should follow behind them. We agreed that if they saw anyone, they would sing a song as a signal to lay down in the hole. We progressed slowly and very cautiously towards the village. We crossed the broken bridge, and increased our pace a little as we neared Trufimyuck's home. He took me to the attic and suggested that I go to sleep.

In the morning Trufimyuck's father called and asked me about many things. Szurko invited me into the house. It consisted of a small room. His sick mother was confined to bed. His younger brother and Yura Niticuk were present, too. They greeted me warmly. We talked about many things while we had breakfast. The conversation turned to the subject of Jews who were waging a bitter struggle for survival. After we ate, Szurko pointed to a corner and said, "If anyone should knock, sit there quietly. Don't cough or moan. At night you will sleep above the oven where it is warm. I will disinfect your clothes immediately. Later we will see what else has to be done."

Like with Trufimyuck was much easier. I sat in the corner all day. His mother questioned me and apprised me of everything that was happening. She was a very progressive woman and she encouraged me. Szurko, who was very intelligent, tried to occupy me with some diversions in his free time. He brought newspapers, and at night we played chess. He kept me from dwelling on my misery and carried on discussions with me for many hours.

He did not get along with his father who was a simple person and a leading anti-Semite. He made sure that Szurko knew about it, too. In the middle of the night, I inadvertently heard him saying, "Father, if I find out that you told anyone about Mechel's being here, then you know what will happen to you. It will be very bad." The words surprised me. The father was afraid of his son but at the same time, respected him immensely. Szurko warned him not to talk with me at length because I knew what he was. Trufimyuck suggested that I visit Czajko to talk.

On January 16, 1944 at night we did go there, and were received very warmly. We sat and talked, nothing unusual. We discussed the gangs and how wantonly they were murdering people. When they caught Jews or Poles, they would ask them to stick out their tongues, which they would then cut off. Or they would remove sex organs and other parts of the bodies. It was unbelievable that a human would act like that. Hearing about it grieved me deeply and it was much more difficult to bear than before. The political situation had changed. Hitler's armies were retreating. Freedom could be proclaimed any day now. In order to avenge the innocent, we had to revitalize ourselves. At night we returned home.

Trufimyuck's life proceeded normally. The most serious problem was the gangs. First there were the Jews, then the Poles, now the Russians and the Communists. We heard about an attack that took place during the night on a family that the gang suspected. They completely annihilated them. Trufimyuck suggested that we dig a bunker in which to hide at any time. We started to burrow a tunnel from the house to the yard outside. We worked ceaselessly. We took the earth from the buckets, put it in the barn and covered it with straw.

On February 11 Trufimyuck brought the news. Russian partisans had come to the villages and forests. The news lent credulity to the belief that the day of liberation was at hand. The delay was occasioned by the fact that they were still far away. To move now was out of the question. Trufimyuck's good friends warned him that the gang could attack on any night and destroy him on the suspicion of his communist affiliation. The people with whom he was associated were considered progressive and communist. Szurko realized that it would be suicidal to remain at home. He sent his family away. But what about me? We discussed my situation. I suggested going to different peasants. He would not hear of it. His argument was,

Life in the Forests and Liberation   209

"Liberation will come in a few days. Now you want to go to the peasants who drank your blood?! Because in holding you now, they believed that they would atone for their sins!" We decided to go to Kostikiewicz. Trufimyuck asked him. He returned with word that he was ready to allow me to stay with him.

On February 13 we called on Kostikiewicz. He received me cordially and I hid in the attic. He gave me a few items of wearing apparel. Every evening Trufimyuck came to visit me. We talked for many hours. Kostikiewicz brought a newspaper but he refused to show it to me. Trufimyuck's response was, "What does it matter? What's the difference between being gassed or being shot? Shooting was worse because people had preknowledge of this method, but gassing was usually unexpected." They told me and showed me evidence that the Germans used gas chambers and that they planned to gas and burn every Jew. They would make soap from the fat. The conversation about the methods Hitler used to achieve his murderous objectives for a nation, continued for a long time.

Kostikiewicz brought regards from Aaron Schwartz, who stayed with him. He knew where Motel Wallach and the Lichter brothers were, too.

On February 21 we noticed German units marching back and forth. They came to Kostikiewicz's house. We discussed the situation with Trufimyuck and decided that I should go back to him, for as long as there were Germans around, the gangs would not attack.

On February 22 I returned to Trufimyuck. Due to the German restriction against venturing out at night and the large mounds of snow, we had difficulties. Every moment something new would take place. Life was hazardous. As the German army left, the gangs came. It was not easy to learn what was happening.

On March 21 fear of staying with Trufimyuck forced me to go to Vassily's house, but I could not stay there because his family became fearful.

On March 24 I made an attempt to stay with Lukujan. Trufimyuck told me that he had agreed. We went there at night. Getting there was very difficult. We had to pass through the snow-covered fields in the presence of the ubiquitous German army. It was the Germans' second front line. Lights focused on us from everywhere and often machine gunfire followed us. We arrived there tired and promptly fell asleep. At daybreak we had breakfast and separated. Trufimyuck promised to visit me in two days. It was hard to stay at Lukujan's, since it was near the forest and the Germans would frequent the area. Lukujan showed me a closet and other furnishings, "All this belongs to Yitzhak Pechornik." He spoke with emotion. "He is somewhere. Peasants say that they saw him wandering in the forest with his wife, Batia, and his child covered in a pillow." Lukujan's daughters were present at all our talks. When the father left the room, the younger daughter, twenty-five-year-old educated Nadia, told me that she had known me for many years and was aware of what I went through. Then she said that she would like to marry me. Shocked, I answered that I was sick, broken and without any plans for the immediate future. (This was added later.)

On March 26 Trufimyuck arrived and said, "We decided that you should return to Vassily at this point. Later we will see what else we can do."

Life in the Forests and Liberation 211

On April 1 at night as we walked, I asked Trufimyuck to visit Czajko. I had a matter I wanted to discuss with him. After a long discussion, Trufimyuck said we would visit the doctor who lived in Yecheskel's house. Maybe he would permit us to stay in his house for a few days. Trufimyuck returned with the doctor's agreement. We were courteously received. At night I slept on the main floor. During the following day I stayed in the attic. All the time there, I would look out through the cracks. The Germans were shooting and roaming about. It was becoming apparent that liberation could come at any moment. The attic was filled with items from Yecheskel's days. They were mementos of Jewish life. It pained me greatly, especially because of the imminent liberation, to realize that what was left of past Jewish life was crammed in some attic.

On April 4 Trufimyuck came, shook my hand and imparted the good news. "I will get you together with another Jew, Aaron Schwartz. But not today. I only came to let you know." His words were most encouraging.

On April 7 Trufimyuck arrived and asked me to join him. Aaron Schwartz was at Kostikiewicz's. We went there quickly. When we got there, Trufimyuck entered the house alone, and then called me in. Aaron Schwartz was there. When he saw me, he looked as if he were lost. Suddenly, he started to cry and I followed suit. He hugged me. "You're alive?" We took a few minutes to look at each other, then Aaron shouted, "Oh, how terribly we struggle. It is impossible to comprehend." We talked about the times past. Aaron asked me how his wife and child were before the slaughter. He cried continually. "My loved ones, my dear loved ones."

We talked about our lives in the fields and forests. We repeated things over and over again. Every Jew who escaped the slaughter suffered just as we did. It was not easy to write down or to listen to our sad history. We, for our own part, were incapable of fully understanding our situation. From the thousands of nomads in fields and forests, only a comparatively few survived. Who knows how long they lived after the war? Every time Aaron talked, I was pained. I could not say anything. Aaron spoke like a child, unburdening his feelings about our tragedy. He removed dirt and lice from his body as if they were minor inconveniences. His words affected me deeply. I suffered through all that time after I left the group, but there was no one to feel or truly understand my pain. Physically we die only once, but we, the few Jews who were persecuted everywhere, spiritually died many times throughout our ordeal. He spoke about a group of 11 Jews in Linave who were originally from Poryck, Torezyn, and Horochow. The shots seemed to come from everywhere. It was impossible to determine the outcome.

On April 9 Trufimyuck came to inform us that the front line of the shelling was only 8 kilometers away and beyond that were the Russians. He said, "I think that if we go to Korytnytsia, we will be close to the Russians. At night we will head for Korytnytsia. I know where the Germans are. Let's hope that we pass the front line without being caught."

At 2:00 AM we started on our way. It was tough going. There was light everywhere. The German rockets illuminated the entire area. With a great deal of difficulty we reached Avross. Happily, he hugged me. "My child, you will live, my dear child." I told him that Aaron Schwartz was outside. He walked out, and all four of us sat down, talking under the straw. Trufimyuck embraced me, "I am finished. I have nothing more to say. I think you understand everything." We kissed. I felt his tears. This energetic man almost made me shake for the first time. He was weak in my arms. After a few minutes, he left. If a history were written about people who fully understood these times, the first award for selflessness would have to be awarded to Trufimyuck. He was a peasant's son, born in 1917, and only reached the 7th grade, but he was very intelligent. Under the Russian occupation he was a school teacher.

Life with Avross was difficult. The Germans were everywhere. The shooting did not cease. We were on the front line.

On April 16 Avross told us that the Germans were seizing young people and taking them away. He said, "The front may be there for a long time. Tonight we will cross to the Russian side. I will not go to church, although it is Paskha (Easter). Be ready." We waited impatiently for the night.

When it came, Avross took us into the forest. He said he would go first alone and that we should follow. We walked quickly. Everything was on schedule. We did not mind being netted in the bushes. We walked that way for a few hours, while shooting continued in the distance. Light projectors illuminated our way and eased our progress. Avross suggested that we rest, and we sat.

The sun started to rise. He pointed to the open field, "This is the village of Postymit, which is occupied by the Russians. When the lights go out, go straight ahead and I will return." Avross hugged me. He cried, "From now on, you are my child. I saved you. I helped you more than most fathers could." Aaron cried and kissed him. It was hard for me to say anything. I felt weak and sad. I had no words to answer. I did not feel the tears streaming. Avross knew. He continued, "Yes, I know your heart. I know how lonely you are. Now you will feel even more painful. But don't worry. You still have a sister (in the USA) and a brother (in Argentina) and many Jews in the world. They will receive you with open arms and happy hearts. The world will then learn everything about you. What happened to your brothers and sisters and how you suffered in the fields and forests. I must leave now. I don't want anything from you. Let God reward me. He knows what I did for you. Take this package and go. Be well. Go, go, my child. Write, from wherever you are." He left.

We sat on the trunk of a felled tree. Aaron was crying. I wanted to calm him, but it was very difficult. When it was light outside, we left. As soon as we entered the field, we heard shouting, "Stand. Raise your hands." A Russian soldier came closer. He asked who we were. He ordered us to take the package and accompany him to headquarters. We were taken to a number of stations. A few officers asked how we survived and if we were German spies. They wanted to

Life in the Forests and Liberation 215

know where we were headed. When we told them it was Lutsk, they freed us.

We walked slowly. Suddenly there was an emptiness in our hearts. Life was suddenly cheap. Our lives passed before our eyes. Aaron talked about everything that was on his mind, and in his heart. About his brother Avrom. He cried bitterly when he remembered how his hands froze and with his gasping breath cried, "I would like to survive, I would like to survive." Aaron said, "I could not help him." The machine guns put an end to our plans.

It was getting dark. We reached the village of Neswic. We had to remain there overnight. We decided to stay among the armed forces. We neared a group of soldiers. I told them that we wanted to stay close by. He advised me to talk to the officer who was astride a horse. I approached him, "Officer, we should like to stay the night not far from here." He asked who we were. "Jews." "Jews! I will bring you to your brother." We all went to a peasant's home. Inside, on a produce magazine, sat another officer. He went over to him and shouted, "I got you two brothers!" The first officer left. We talked with the Jewish soldier in Yiddish. He told us that he was from Wynice and said, "My family was liquidated like all the others." We all spoke about our destruction. He gave us some canned food and something to smoke. He took us outside among the soldiers in the barn. He announced that, until the following day, we would stay there with them. He said that tomorrow he would send us to Lutsk, and only there because that's where all the Jews would gather. There we should decide what to do. As far as he had learned, there were 60 Jews in Lutsk.

It was a very tiresome night. Our sleep was disturbed by our thoughts. At the first sign of light, two soldiers entered. They asked, "Where are the two Jews?" The Jewish officer also came. He gave us two small packages and bade us a friendly good-bye. We left.

We climbed on the back of the vehicle that took us to Lutsk. The town was in a turmoil. Soldiers and officers were everywhere. We wandered through the street, asking where we could find Jews. While walking, we met Yitzhak Zuker from Horochow. Very happily we opened up and talked. He told us that there were some other Jews from Svyniukhy, Shlomo and Yankel Lichter and Motel Wallach in the group of 11 from Linave. In addition, Bairel Kercer from Bluduw was alive and so were the two Dobrowice brothers and Wallach. We went to the group from Linave. Aaron stayed. Bairel Kercer and I called on the Svyniukhy group, the Lichter brothers and Motel Wallach. As we entered, we froze in our tracks, looking at each other. Shlomo broke the silence, asking if I had just arrived. Yankel started to cry and moan, *"Oi vay, oi vay."* We talked. Shlomo and Yankel asked me about everything, mostly about their wives and children, and how they looked before I left the ghetto. The conversation eventually revolved around the last hours of life of our beloved ones.

We talked a great deal about our village and Lukacze and about who survived. From Svyniukhy, there were Yankel Meizlish, his wife and two children and us. From Lukacze, so far, no one. We talked about my group and if anyone knew who was alive, but unfortunately they were no longer among the living. We

Life in the Forests and Liberation 217

looked at each other. How forelorn we seemed. After I left the ghetto, I started losing my hair. At this time it was almost all gone.

Yankel Lichter was heard to describe how terribly broken he was. Shlomo believed that it was almost a certainty that our brothers were gassed and cremated. The killers stooped to every indignity to reach their goals. We all stood with bowed heads and kept silent. We were the poor victims of a horrible tragedy. We were soaked in our own blood and incapable of correctly evaluating our disintegration. Everything seemed like a bad dream. But looking back, I'm horrified once again and my body starts to quiver involuntarily. For each survivor, his or her life and struggle for survival was almost identical with all the other fortunate ones. It was field and/or forest, graves for the living and facing the continuous specter of death.

For future generations, historians will be able to record our tragedy. It is incontrovertably true that the Jews suffered the most losses in the war. Hitler and the German people were responsible. We should never forget it. Generation after generation should learn that we were caged and tortured. How weary, exhausted, isolated and starved we were.

The persistent vision of the blood of our children pouring out of the mass graves. The unbearable pain of the fathers and mothers leading their children to the slaughter. The live skeletons who were wandering like zombies through field and forest, and eventually killed in some unknown place. One thing must remain indelibly etched in our hearts: a perpetual vengeance for our spilled blood.

APPENDIXES

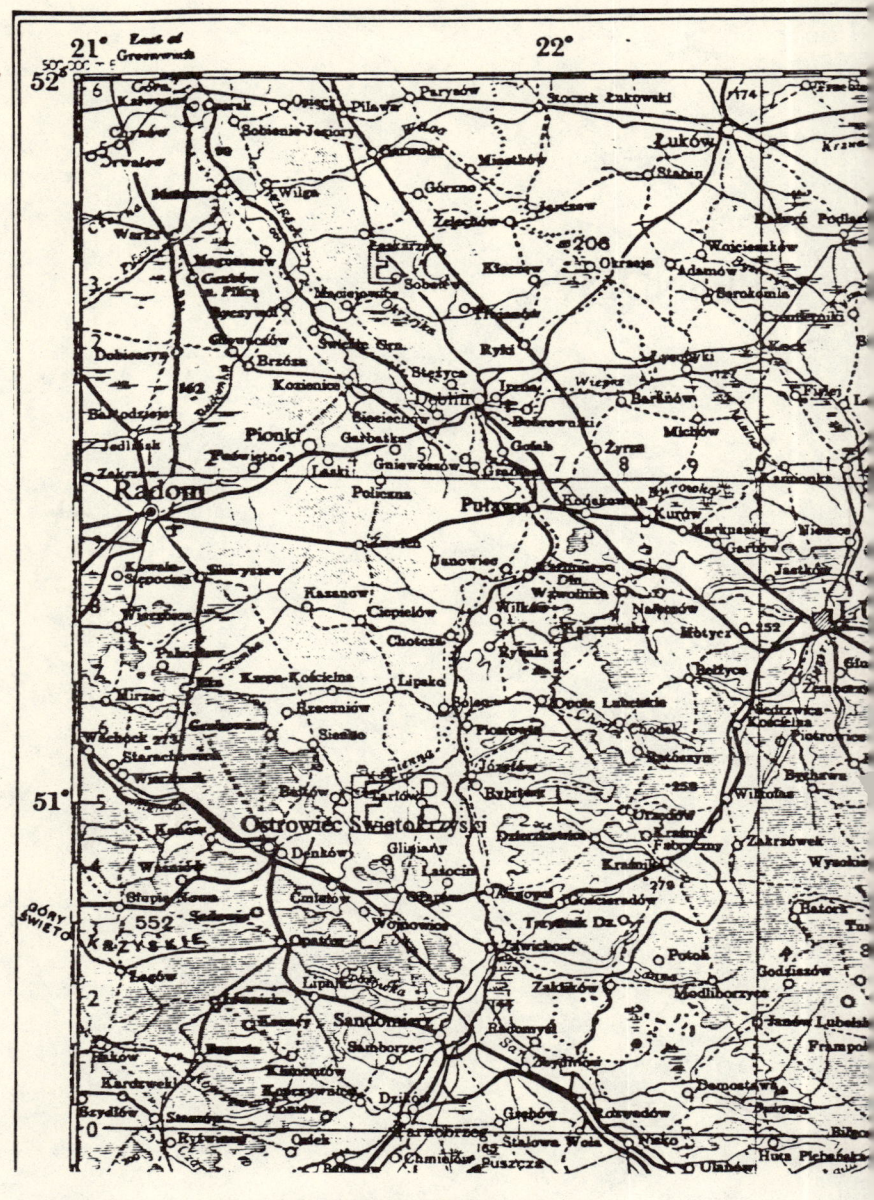

APPENDIX I MAP OF THE REGION

23°
24°
Chotyłów
Kodeń
Medna
Velikorita
Ozero Lukovo
Lubowel
Kanal Turskiy
Komarówka
Wisznice
Hanna
Opole
Mokrany
Malorita
Gorniki
Olitusha
Tur
Ratno
Ozero Turskoye
Zabolot'ye
Pripyat'
Velimche
Pishcha
Włodawa
Dubechnoye
Zamshany
Tomashevka
Pul'mo
Shatsk
Orchówek
Sobibór
Krymno
Lyubokhiny
Włodawka
Ozero Svityaz'skoye
Vyzhevka
Staraya Vyzhevka
Myzovo
Hańsk
Zabuzh'ye
Zgorany
Uhrusk
Opalin
Golovno
Sawin
Gushcha
Lyuboml'
Równo
Świerże
Berezhtsy
Sedliszcze
Pawłów
Chełm
Dorohusk
Uday
Turiysk
Rejowiec
Dubienka
Krasnystaw
Białopole
Korytnitsa
Wojsławice
Uchanie
Verba
Izbica
Ustilug
Vladimir-Volynskiy
Skierbieszów
Grabowiec
Hrubieszów
Khotyachev
Chernikov
Mikulichi
Zamość
Werbkowice
Krylów
Ivanichi
Pavlovka
Żabunie
Komarów
Tyszowce
Krynice
Dołhobyczów
Milyatin
Krasnobród
Łaszczów
Podberez'ye
Tarnawatka
Rachanie
Telatyn
Sokal'

APPENDIX II
THE EVOLUTION OF THE RECORD-KEEPING OF THE DIARY

A short time after the war started, realizing that it might last a long time, I decided to collect information about the conflict. I kept all of my writings in my home. The primary collection of data was made during the war, under very difficult conditions, through daily recordings and the collecting of the factual data.

As soon as I learned that I would have to leave my home and the area of Svyniukhy for the Lukacze ghetto, I sought a safe way to preserve the information I had already gathered and whatever else would be collected in the future.

In order to secure the scraps and notes already in my possession, I turned them over to Czajko, my Ukrainian neighbor. We agreed that if anything happened to me, he would release the collection to a reputable Jewish organization or to a Jew he could trust. Czajko kept gathering all the scraps and notes until two weeks before the slaughter.

I held onto the memorandum I wrote from the period of two weeks prior to the massacre, to the time I left my friends in the forest. Those slips were secured in a *Cerate* (a piece of rubber that is placed under a baby's crib sheet to protect the mattress.) and in a water-proof bag. I gave the wet notes describing the details of the tragedy and life in the forest, to Czajko when I was drenched in the river.

Later, when I stayed in the "grave of the living" on Avross's property, he kept all the scraps in a similar manner that Czajko and I had devised. Avross asked me to allow him to hold on to the materials and not to turn them over to Czajko so that they could prove that, even in the difficult times, he helped.

From Avross I went to Andrii Zilins'kyi. After a few nights with him, I called on Czajko to hand over to him all the bits and pieces.

After wandering about, I visited Trufimyuck. There I had the opportunity to review all the information and there I was able to supplement the collection with a great deal of additional data regarding the past and present.

Four days before the end of the war, I collected all the notes. Trufimyuck's mother made a small bag for me in which to place everything that I could and that I could tie to my body.

After the liberation, I went to the town of Lutsk. There the Russians mobilized me into the Red Army (April 21, 1944). During a physical exercise at the beginning of my military service, the officer in charge noticed the bag around my body and informed the NKVD (secret police). They called me in for interrogation, and ordered me to turn over the bag. I refused but informed them of the contents. They then insisted on inspecting the bag for political materials. They promised to return it in a few days. After 15 days, I was called to the office of a high-ranking officer of the NKVD. He received me cordially, returned the bag with all its contents intact and said, "Save it. It is special information. I hope that you'll survive and go to Moscow to publish it." He gave me a letter from the NKVD officially enjoining anyone from taking it away from me.

After my release from the Red Army, I went to Poland. From there we left for Israel as Greek Jews. In order to preclude possible problems attendant upon the legality of crossing borders, the leaders of the group confiscated all official documents: driver's licenses, identification cards and other materials written in Polish, Russian, or other languages. They took the NKVD letter as well. I never got it back. They asked for my memoranda, too, but I refused to surrender them, warning, "If I have to part with this material, I will not go."

On Cypress, at a checkpoint to the entrance to the camp, the British soldiers once again wanted me to give up the notes. They disallowed the entry of money and written materials into the camp. After a heated argument, they permitted me to keep them.

In a tent on Cypress, by the light of a crude kerosene lamp, I started to put together the diary from my scraps. I finished the task during the first half of 1947.

In this way, the diary was kept in its original state as an authentic, detailed and accurate manuscript, handwritten on 288 pages.

APPENDIX III
EXPLANATION FOR THE DELAY IN PUBLICATION

After the war my main objective was to tell the world about the events in which I participated or knew about. I therefore worked diligently during every free moment to complete the diary, and finally did so in 1947 in Israel.

At that time my wife and I were sharing one room with another family. I worked at two jobs to earn a living. We started to expand our family and during a war was no time to try to publish a diary.

The late forties in Israel may be characterized as a time of impatience with the survivors. I heard prominent leaders, like Dulchin, say, "Yes, we know everything about you, going like sheep to the slaughter." It is not difficult to compare it to the statement by Trufimyuck, "Stay with us. We are the only ones who will understand you."

The fifties were also characterized by a lack of patience towards the Holocaust survivors. They were accused of going meekly to the slaughter without any active resistance. The survivors thought of themselves as standing alone against the enemy. Many people were impatient, unsympathetic, disbelieving, and avoided the survivors. These attitudes of the fifties and late forties spilled over into the sixties. People did not wish to talk about the past. The authorities seemed to believe the canard, "Like sheep to the slaughter." The official policy was to disregard the catastrophe and to get on with the business of regenerating the country. The reparations agreement did not resolve or diminish the problem. The survivor was forced to distance himself or herself from the rest of the people.

During all these years, the sixties, seventies and eighties, I was sick, at times even seriously so.

Attempts to publish the diary were made. The reaction in one case was, "It is not appropriate material for the newspaper reader." In another attempt I was asked to defray the cost of publication, which was beyond my means.

It seemed as if the diary and I were orphaned, or, like Moses, we had to remain in the desert for forty years.